# Welcome

*Your Guide to*
# MODELLING EUROPEAN RAILWAYS
## CM EUROPEAN SPECIAL

We are sure you will enjoy and be inspired by this European Special, our second geographically-themed extra edition. The railways of Europe are, of course, often the subject of the articles in CONTINENTAL MODELLER, but this Special allows us to present longer features, in more detail, and with more and larger pictures than would usually be possible in a regular issue of the magazine. The Special is approximately equivalent to two issues – though for rather less than two issues would cost!

CM has a long tradition of sourcing material and using contributors from Europe, going right back to the very first issue, and we are delighted that one from that time, Guus Veenendaal, is also represented in these pages – still actively modelling, developing the theme that has occupied him all the while. He reports how the layout has moved house and been expanded. We have been privileged to visit the layout both in its old home and its new location, and we take this opportunity to thank Guus and Jannie for their hospitality.

When considering what to include in this guide, we came to the conclusion that the best way to illustrate European modelling was with the work of European modellers, and so all the features are 'authentic', despite a wealth of 'home talent'. (If this special is well received, perhaps we can redress the balance in future with another publication.)

Despite our (in)famous insularity, British modellers are more interested in overseas prototypes than our continental cousins. Most of them follow their local scene, and only admit 'foreign' stock on through services. There are exceptions, of course: the Swiss metre gauge, and in particular the Rhätische Bahn, has a very wide appeal.

But no other country supports so many special interest societies: there are, or have been, groups based in the UK dedicated to the railways of all the major countries in Europe – and quite a few of the minor ones! It may be due to the lack of foreign language skills, which means the societies have an important rôle not only finding sources of information but also translating it.

Even in a dedicated work of this size, we can only hope to provide an introduction, to give a flavour, and to show something of the appeal of modelling European railways. It is a large and varied continent. We have tried to feature a mixture of scales and gauges, and layouts large and small, to cater for all tastes, and resources.

Not least because Europe is so varied, it is difficult, and not particularly useful, to generalise about the railway differences between Europe and Britain: electrification is more widespread, and has been for some time; there have always been significant independent as well as state railways; the recent growth of private operators; and narrow gauge is more widely used – and still as a part of the transport system, not just preserved.

In modelling terms, the techniques, tools, and basic materials are very similar, so we have avoided covering basic ground (almost literally!). As will be seen in some of these features, some British products can be adapted.

There are many specific differences in detail which give each Eureopan railway system its own character. To deal with any of them properly would require separate dedicated publications.

The scales employed span a similar range, although the ratios do differ slightly. TT is more popular than in Britain, especially in the eastern bloc. O has been on the rise in recent years, due in no small part to Lenz. (Some European O is 1:43.5, as in Britain, while 1:45 is favoured in Germany and Switzerland.) There is also increasing interest in Gauge 1. G ranges now include standard gauge prototypes which are closer to Gauge 1. (G is nominally 1:22.5 but commercial products are 'flexible' – the Germans say that G stands for Gummi, elastic!)

Reflecting the prototype situation, certain narrow gauge subjects have more commercial support.

In most markets, there have been fewer 'kits and bits' suppliers than in Britain, and this number is declining further as more and more is produced ready-to-run, even for smaller country prototypes.

Digital control was developed and more widely accepted earlier in Europe, albeit originally as separate and incompatible systems from the major brands.

The continued prominence of the three-rail AC system from Märklin also seems strange to many British modellers.

As might be expected, such a large and vibrant market is well supported with magazines and books, and internet sites.

European material is easily available from several specialist outlets in Britain, most of whom advertise regularly in CONTINENTAL MODELLER.

So, here is a selective look at European modelling – we trust that you find it interesting and entertaining.

## A brief guide to the 'Epoch/Era' dating system

As a convenient way of defining broad periods of railway history across Europe, the following terms are generally used:

EPOCH I – approximately 1870 to 1920;
   vehicles in the liveries of the separate state and private railways.
EPOCH II – approximately 1920 to 1945,
   from the formation of the large national state networks
   (DRG, BBÖ, SBB, etc).
EPOCH III – approximately 1945 to 1968.
EPOCH IV – approximately 1968 to 1994;
   vehicles with UIC computer numbering.
EPOCH V – 1994 to 2006, from the foundation of DBAG,
   the formation of private railway operating companies
   and Europe-wide liberalisation of railway traffic.
EPOCH VI – introduction of new Europe-wide UIC vehicle numbers
   containing a country-specific code, starting 2007.

## Scale and gauge comparison

| | UK | gauge (model) | Europe | | gauge represented |
|---|---|---|---|---|---|
| Z | 1:220 | 6.5mm | 1:220 | Z | standard |
| no equivalent | | 6.5mm | 1:160 | Nm | metre |
| N | 1:148 | 9mm | 1:160 | N | standard |
| TT | 1:100 | 12mm | 1:120 | TT | standard |
| OO | 1:76 | 16.5mm | 1:87 | HO | standard |
| no equivalent | | 6.5mm | 1:87 | HOf | 60cm |
| OO9 | 1:76 | 9mm | 1:87 | HOe | 75/76cm |
| OOn3 | 1:76 | 12mm | 1:87 | HOm | metre |
| O | 1:43.5 | 32mm | 1:45 | O | standard |
| O-16.5 | 1:43.5 | 16.5mm | 1:45 | Oe | 75/76cm |
| no equivalent | | 22.2mm | 1:45 | Om | metre |
| 1 | 1:32 | 45mm | 1:32 | 1 | standard |
| G | 1:22.5 | 45mm | 1:22.5 | G | metre |

**PECO**
MODELLERS' LIBRARY

*Your Guide to*
**MODELLING EUROPEAN RAILWAYS**

## CM EUROPEAN SPECIAL

62

36

6

# Contents

72

84

118 76

| | |
|---|---|
| **Editor** | Andrew Burnham |
| **Assistant Editor** | Tim Rayner |
| **Associate Editor & Photographer** | |
| | Steve Flint |
| **Editorial Assistant & Photographer** | |
| | Craig Tiley |
| **Editorial Assistant** | Ingrid Rose |
| **Art Director** | Adrian Stickland |
| **Graphic Illustration** | Brian Meredith, |
| Dave Clements, Gary Bickley, David Malton | |
| **General & Advertisement Manager** | |
| | John King |
| **Direct Subscriptions** | Alicia Knight |
| **Editorial Director** | Ben Arnold |

Printed by William Gibbons & Sons Ltd., P.O.Box 103, 26, Planetary Road, Willenhall, West Midlands, WV13 3XT.

ISBN 9780900586057          ref.PM-205

© Peco Publications & Publicity Ltd. 2016

# A classic continental home layout design

# Neustadt

**Stephan Rieche** reports on the layout built by Horst Losacker
to recall the post-war age of steam in Germany, with detailed locomotives.
*Photographs by the author.*

Horst Losacker is among the few modellers who experienced the railways when they were still using steam locomotives in regular service. Creating a miniature memorial to the black thoroughbreds was his intention with this layout, the central feature of which is a medium-sized depot.

He wanted to convey the fascination he got from steam locomotives in the model. After all, in his youth he had seen the heavy class 44s from Bw Gelsenkirchen-Bismarck, the fleet-footed 03 Pacifics from Köln-Deutz, and the ubiquitous 50s that were useful everywhere. So the choice of the layout theme was not difficult – a running shed. Since this on it own is not so interesting to operate, a small station was also planned.

The available area was 3.2m by 2.7m, in which the layout could be built in an L-shape. So one side houses the depot and the other accommodates Neustadt station. This gives the impression of a through station because originally an extension was planned but in fact it is a terminus.

As the trains therefore have to reverse direction, then they also get a new locomotive. This provides a justification for the presence of the depot. Further, the locomotive changes,

Below
**A BR56 2-8-0 is by the sand tower, behind that a BR66 2-6-4T moves towards the water cranes, and on the right a BR64 2-6-2T is being coaled.**

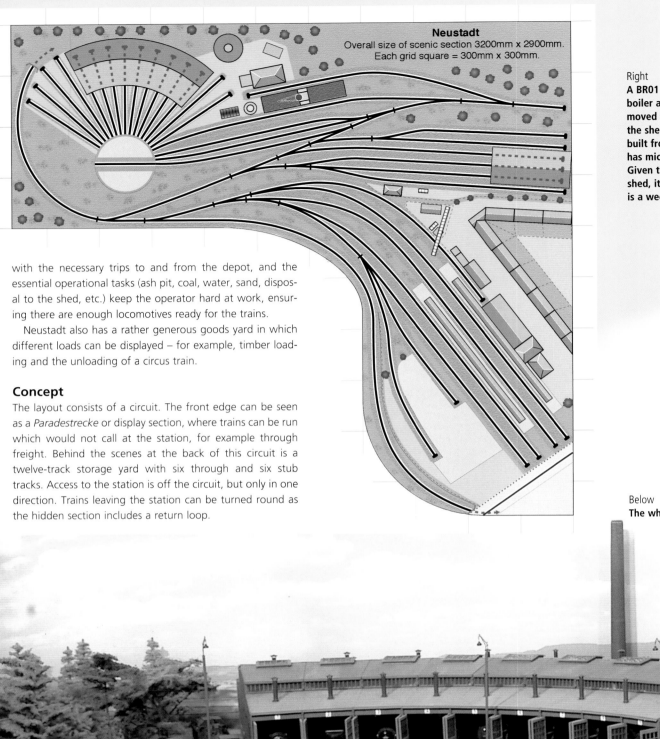

**Neustadt**
Overall size of scenic section 3200mm x 2900mm.
Each grid square = 300mm x 300mm.

Right
A BR01 Pacific with the old boiler and front skirt is moved by the turntable into the shed. The model was built from a Weinert kit and has micro LEDs in the lamps. Given the many locos on shed, it seems likely that it is a weekend.

with the necessary trips to and from the depot, and the essential operational tasks (ash pit, coal, water, sand, disposal to the shed, etc.) keep the operator hard at work, ensuring there are enough locomotives ready for the trains.

Neustadt also has a rather generous goods yard in which different loads can be displayed – for example, timber loading and the unloading of a circus train.

## Concept

The layout consists of a circuit. The front edge can be seen as a *Paradestrecke* or display section, where trains can be run which would not call at the station, for example through freight. Behind the scenes at the back of this circuit is a twelve-track storage yard with six through and six stub tracks. Access to the station is off the circuit, but only in one direction. Trains leaving the station can be turned round as the hidden section includes a return loop.

Below
The whole of the loco depot.

## Baseboard and track

The foundation is an open frame construction. The rear section is open, covered by a removable forest. Horst Losacker admits to an error with this, which he advises other modellers to avoid: he applied too much plaster and the piece became so heavy that it is very difficult to handle. It would have been better make the removable piece from foam materials.

The track is mostly Roco Line, but painted rust colour and ballasted.

**Above**
Waiting near the engine shed are a super-detailed Fleischmann BR94 0-10-0T, which has new lamps, brake hoses, and extra pipework, and a BR64 2-6-2T built from a Weinert kit. The subtle weathering of the locomotives should be noted.

**Below**
The BR66 2-6-4T (Lenz) is being filled with sand – obviously a process which often results in spills. Behind, the emergency coaling crane is ready for action.

**Right**
A small locomotive by the large coal stage: a BR24 2-6-0 (another super-detailed Fleischmann model) is being coaled.

**Right**
A BR41 2-8-2 (Weinert) by the water crane. Note the open water hatches into which a perspex rod was hooked to imitate the water. In the background is the depot administration building.

Right
**Against the backdrop of the diesel shed, a BR64 2-6-2T (Weinert) arrives at the station with a train of *Donnerbüchsen* (Thunderboxes) as long timber is loaded in the goods yard.**

Above

A busy moment at the steam depot: in front a BR41 2-8-2 (Weinert) takes water, behind a BR86 2-8-2T (Weinert) waits to be coaled.
On the rear track coal wagons are being unloaded.

Right

By the goods shed there is a fuel merchant and a building materials yard which is receiving load of steel girders.

Below

Old boiler BR01 Pacific at the coal stage.

Above
A panoramic view of Neustadt station. A fast train has just arrived, and a shunter will be required to release the loco as all the platform tracks are simple dead ends.
On the near track, a BR86 waits to depart with the train of Thunderboxes.

Left
In the diesel depot a V200 is being refueled, while there is apparently no space in the modern shed for the V100. A work train is parked in the background.

Right
A fast train headed by a BR38 4-6-0 (built from a Weinert kit) is about to start from the station and is waiting for the signal. On the neighbouring platform travellers wait for their train.

## Backscene and buildings

With such a relatively small layout, it is important to make it look larger than it is, so a suitable backscene is essential. Horst Losacker used the modular printed backdrops by MZZ (unfortunately no longer produced) which were easy to adapt to a specific layout. The houses in the urban scenes as printed match the kits used particularly well, giving a harmonious overall impression.

The buildings in the small town and the railway structures are all from the ranges of the usual manufacturers – Kibri, Faller, Pola, etc. However, they were all repainted with Revell colours and subtly weathered to take away the plastic sheen. The coaling plant, the ash pit, and the sanding tower are by Bochmann and Kochendörfer: unfortunately, this excellent range of loco depot accessories is no longer available. Happy the man who has – or manages to find – such a kit!

## Rolling stock

The layout is set in Era III, the 1950s. Steam locomotives still dominate the depot, but modern diesels are beginning to appear – the diesel shed has been found a place between the station and the steam depot.

Horst Losacker leaves few locomotives as they come out of the box. Those from the major manufacturers get at least a decent detailed buffer beam and scale-size, free-standing lamps, missing pipes are replaced, and the locos get a new coat of paint and a subtle weathering. The installation of a Faulhaber motor is now taken for granted. He has also greatly enjoyed assembling many Weinert locomotive kits because of the good fit of the parts and the excellent detailing.

Below
**The passenger train has been taken over by a BR86 2-8-2T (Weinert). The BR64 2-6-2T is waiting for the train to leave the station so that it can run to the shed.**

**Right**
The circus is in town! In the 1950s, circuses still travelled from city to city by train. A BR81 0-8-0T (Weinert) shunts the wagons (Roco) onto the different sidings in the goods yard. The circus models are by Preiser.

**Right**
Unloading the circus caravans in the goods yard. Note also that some of the stake-sided flat cars have the end walls folded down to demonstrate unloading at the end dock.

**Below right**
The bridge over the station provides an excellent view of the goods yard and the platforms. But if you want to take a look at the loco depot, you will need binoculars, like the railway enthusiast in front of the passenger train!

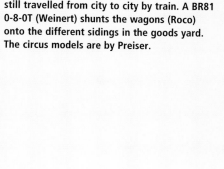

## A possible subject to model, once with interesting goods traffic

# Buxtehude

**Benno Wiesmüller** describes an interesting station in northern Germany.

*Drawings and photographs by the author, or from his collection.*

With the opening of the first section of the Unterelbische Eisenbahngesellschaft's line from Hamburg-Harburg to Stade on 1st April 1881, Buxtehude was served by rail. The whole 103km route to Cuxhaven was opened on 11th November 1881, initially as single track.

Building had been postponed due to the annexation of Hannover by Prussia and the fact that the Cuxhaven Railway, Steamship, and Port Joint Stock Company had to sell its share of the state railway concession to a Belgian railway company, for financial reasons. The Unterelbische company was then founded in Berlin, and construction got under way again.

The station buildings along the route (Unterelbe, Neugraben, Buxtehude, Horneburg, Stade, Himmelpforten, Hechthausen, Basbeck-Ost, Cadenberge, Neuhaus a d Oste, Otterndorf, Altenbruch, and Cuxhaven) were, although different in size, largely all built in the same style. There were (and still are) identical buildings on certain lines in Belgium, built following the same plans.

The station building (EG) was arranged parallel to the tracks, with sections of different length on the single storey part of the building, usually with a two-storey section at one end. The building in Buxtehude later got a three metre exten-

Above
**Buxtehude station c.1906.**

Below
**A view of the site c.1910.**
Photos: Stadtarchiv Buxtehude.

sion at the eastern end. In 1905, an upper storey was added to most of the old building.

The initial service consisted of one mixed and two passenger trains each day. The following year, an express train with connections to Helgoland and a Sunday special train were added.

In 1889 the regular HAPAG special trains began on the Hamburg – Cuxhaven route, transporting passengers to and from the overseas steamers. Up to the start of the First World War, many emigrants left Germany by this route.

In May 1902, the entire route was converted to double track.

Buxtehude station consisted of two main through tracks – track I was the main platform and track II had a single-sided sandy platform. On the south side there was the *Ladestraße* (goods yard), served by track 5 which was connected at both ends to the two main tracks. (The main tracks were at that period designated by Roman numerals, the sidings with Arabic.)

On the north side of the site were, from east to west, the eastern signal box (Bo), a neighbouring building, the station building, a loading dock, a shed, a water tower, the goods shed, the northern goods yard, and the western signal box (Bw). North of track I, between the station building and the

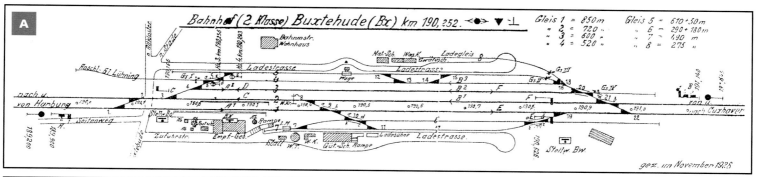

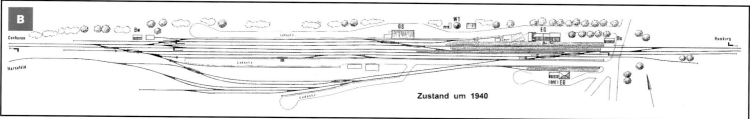

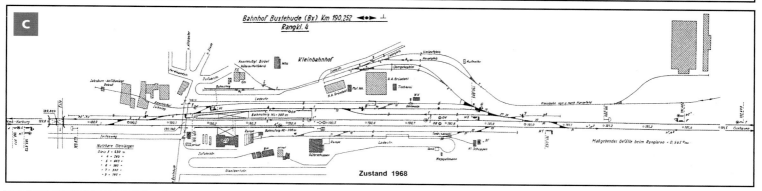

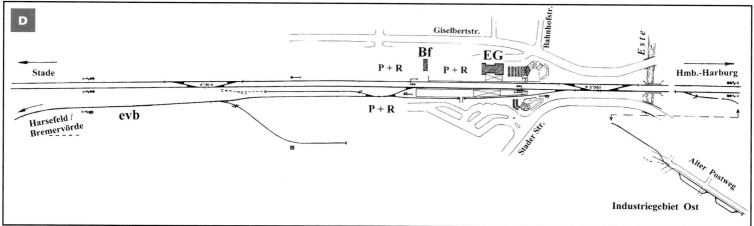

Above

**The changing track plan at Buxtehude.**

A 1928
B 1940
C 1968
D present day

**NB diagrams not to scale.**

western signal box, were tracks 7 (wagon stabling siding) and 8 (loading track). This latter ended with a side and end loading dock; a few metres further to the west there was a weighbridge. By the goods shed there were two diamond crossings and two plain points connecting track II and track 8; near the western signal box a similar link ran from track II over track I to tracks 7 and 8.

Between the 1890s and the beginning of the First World War, the layout of the station was expanded. Overtaking track III was added between track II and 5, and soon after there was an addition to track 5. All three tracks (III, 4, and 5) ran from the east signal box (Bo) to the point by the west box (Bw), i.e. the entire length of the station.

As exit signals in the Hamburg direction there were two adjacent semaphore signals, the higher for track II (Hs1) and the lower for track III (Hs2). Exit signals E and F were at the Stade end. While the exit signals at that time all had only one arm, the entry signals (A from Hamburg, B from Stade) were equipped with two in order to display the signal aspects Hp1 and Hp2.

Incidentally, the Lühning company's siding had been added by 1912.

Apart from the points by the west box connecting to the Buxtehude – Harsefelder Eisenbahn (BHE), the track layout hardly changed until the 1960s.

It was similar with the buildings. In the first decade a post

shed was added between the toilet block and the station
building, in the area of the water tower more storage sheds
and a toilet, by the goods shed a loading platform and ramp,
and west of the west signal box a loco shed.

Drawings reproduced to 1:160 (N).

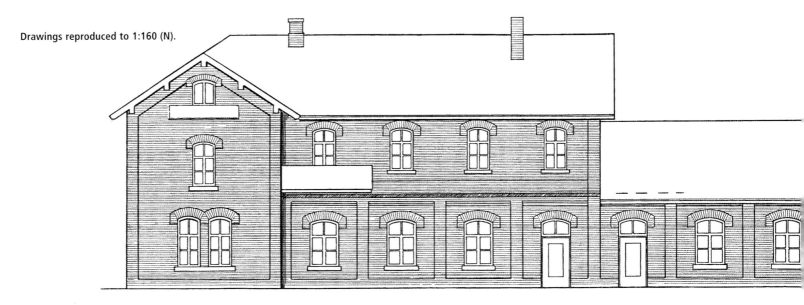

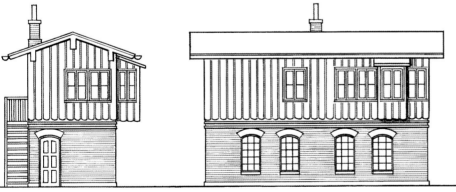

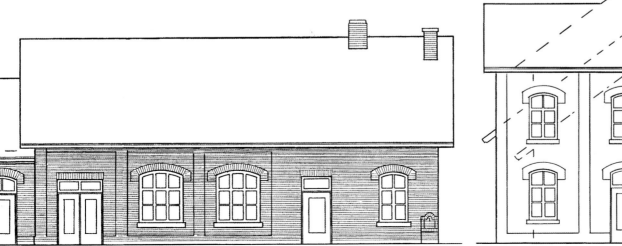

Other minor changes were, among others, moving the weighbridge from track 7 to track 5, extending the east box to 9.45m long, and rebuilding track 4 for arrivals from the direction of Stade. For this protective stop signals (Hs 3 and 4) were placed at the east end of tracks 3 and 4. According to the former signal system, the entry signal from Stade was given a third arm (Hp0 = Halt, Hp1 = running into or through track 2, Hp2 = run to track 3, Hp3 = run to track 4). So Buxtehude had two passing loops available, track 3 for both directions and track 4 for trains to Hamburg.

**Left**
Controlling signal box Bf,
formerly Buxtehude West,
and the shed for small locos,
22nd June 1975.

**Below left**
Signal box Bf, formerly Bw,
7th May 1985.
Note the loco shed has gone.

**Right**
The replacement signal box
Bf, now remotely operated
from Hamburg-Neugraben.
July 2001.

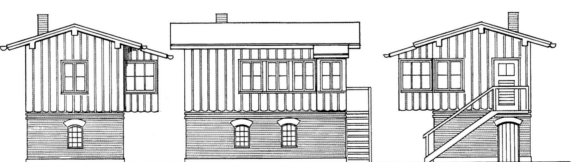

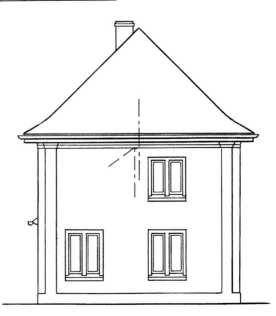

Incidentally, the engine shed west of the west signal box was already by 1928 without track.

On the south side of the railway yard, on the hill opposite the station building, the Unterelbische Brewery was opened in 1890; it had its own refrigerated vans. In 1918 the mill owner Hastedt acquired the brewery and transformed it into a pasta factory. In 1936 the company was taken over by the Birkel brothers.

After years of delay, the Buxtehude – Harsefeld light railway, founded in 1913, opened the almost 15km long route on 19th December 1928. The station building was a massive two-storey brick building with a hipped roof; on the west end was a goods shed with a gable roof. A two-track loco shed was planned for the west end of the site but never built. The main track ended at the platform, and there were two transfer tracks, a storage siding, a run-round loop, and a loading siding.

To simplify shunting and shorten the time goods trains had to wait at intermediate stations, the DRG acquired small internal combustion engined locomotives. Such a machine was stationed in Buxtehude from 1931, and a small wooden shed was put up to house it just east of the west signal box.

Left
**A Buxtehude – Harsefeld Eisenbahn mixed train at Buxtehude Süd, 24th December 1956. The loco is 0-6-0T No.352, former Wilstedt – Zeven – Tostedt Eisenbahn No.1 (Hanomag 7651 of 1915), sold to the BHE in 1955.**
Photo: H.Hoyer.

**Buxtehude Süd station building. Drawings reproduced to 1:160 (N).**

It must be noted that even before the First World War there was brisk Sunday traffic, with the thousands of day-trippers from Hamburg visiting Buxtehude and the surrounding area. That brought the station staff a lot of extra work.

In 1940 the Estekaserne (Este barracks) was completed and Buxtehude became a garrison town, and the station saw significant extra military traffic. Five storage sidings with a locomotive shed and workshop were planned for west of the west signal box, but never built.

Major damage to buildings and equipment by enemy air raids only occurred during the last days of the war, on 18th April 1945 when Allied bombers attacked an anti-aircraft train standing in the station area. Parts of the Birkel company, a residential building, the station building, and some of the track was affected. Track from Giselbertsraße and Brünningstraße as far as Victoria-Luise-Straße was damaged. Twelve people lost their lives, and many were injured. On 22nd April 1945, Buxtehude was surrendered without a fight to British troops. They occupied the barracks for the next ten years. In 1957 it was transferred to the Bundeswehr and remained in use until 1994.

In the early post-war years the few trains that ran were crammed with people from the city who wanted to trade in the country everyday objects or valuables for food. More or less successful, they returned to the station, if necessary even riding on the running boards, the buffers, or the roof to get home – these were the infamous 'hamster trains'.

The Kleinbahn Buxtehude – Harsefeld (after 1942 known as the Buxtehude – Harsefelder Railway, or BHE) could not resume operating until May 1946 because its running line was blocked with damaged standard gauge wagons. To avoid confusion, its station had meanwhile been renamed 'Buxtehude South'.

In the 1950s, among other things, the slips in the main lines were replaced by simple crossovers.

The passenger trains timetabled to stop at Buxtehude, then called passenger and fast trains, consisted mainly of six-wheel third class compartment coaches or four-wheel second class vehicles, a six-wheel or bogie baggage van, and a post van. The express trains were later formed

with steel coaches of riveted construction, often hauled by class 38 steam locomotives at first then from the early 1950s mainly the BR03 light Pacifics.

From 1943 to the early 1950s the double-deck trains of the former Lübeck – Buchener Eisenbahn ran from Hamburg through Buxtehude, hauled by the partially streamlined class 74 locomotives.

From the early 1960s passenger trains (later referred to as regional trains) were increasingly made up of 'Silverfish' coaches working as push-pull sets with V100 diesel locomotives, while the express services were for many years still made up of pre-war fast train stock still hauled until the latter part of the 1960s for the most part by steam locomotives.

The BHE began operation with secondhand steam locomotives. By May 1933, a four-wheel Wismar railcar was used for passenger services. It was later rebuilt and ran from 1955 to 1965 as T104 between Buxtehude and Harsefeld.

For economy, the BHE only bought secondhand vehicles. Four bogie railcars were acquired between 1952 and 1962: one fell victim to a fire, and two were damaged in level crossing accidents with lorries in 1962 and 1965 and had to be

Above
**Buxtehude goods shed, 7th May 1985.**

scrapped. Only T175 remained and after the withdrawal of passenger traffic in 1969 it was used to haul freight trains. In 1979/80 it was overhauled as museum pieces and can still be seen now and again in Buxtehude.

For the last four years of passenger traffic, in 1965 the BHE acquired a first series Uerdinger railbus from the Lübeck – Segeberger railway.

Around 1960, the west signal box was converted to be the

main signal box in place of the former command post in the station building. The head signalman, who previously also supervised the trains and gave the departure authority with his red cap and command staff, now worked from the west box (later redesignated Bf). For supervising trains and sending them on their way there now had to be an inspector on the station, naturally with red cap and command staff! Later responsibility was transferred to the train crew, but an inspector still had to be present on the platform. During the night he also had to take over the ticket office and the baggage handling.

As part of the electrification works, instead of the two single side sand platforms on tracks 2 and 3, accessible only by level crossings, a fixed central platform with a pedestrian underpass was installed. In addition, both the new central platform and the main platform got canopies. Track 3 had to be changed and track 4 shortened. The double slips were replaced with simple crossovers. The connection to the goods shed between track 2 and track 8 was also removed.

Electric operation between Hamburg-Harburg and Stade was introduced on 24th September 1968.

**Drawings reproduced to 1:160 (N).**

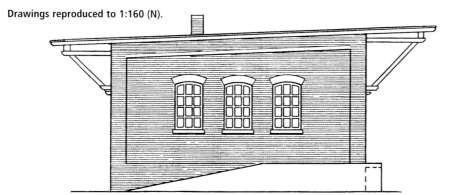

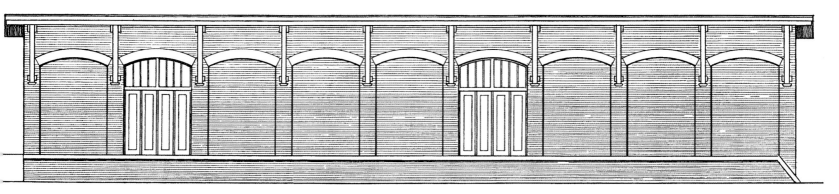

## Busy with freight

As well as wagonload freight, at this period Buxtehude still had a lot small packet business, in and out, which was loaded and unloaded in the goods shed. Packets without the endorsement "to be collected" were delivered to the recipients by the 'official railway carrier'. Until the early 1960s this was still partly done with the typical horse-drawn carts.

At the loading points mainly agricultural products were handled. Incoming were mainly fertilisers and fuels (coal and oil). In the autumn, there was significant extra traffic in sugar beet, potatoes, and apples, most of which came off the BHE and was transferred to the DB in Buxtehude.

In addition, the northern goods yard loading track was equipped with a transfer dock for road trailers on which rail wagons could be transported to companies without sidings. In Buxtehude companies including Granini and Klintworth received wagons in this way. For large volumes, two of these special railway-owned road vehicles could be used together. The two short pieces of track used to hold the wagons at the Klintworth company – today Rederei NSB – only disappeared in the middle of the last decade with the re-arrangement of the area.

Also, near the end of the northern loading area, the Heppelman storage company had tanks for diesel fuel and heating oil.

Among the companies with a rail connection were the Birkel pasta factory, who had their own silo wagons (type Ucs) for conveying powdered goods, as well as the Lühning timber company; via their siding the bone processing company Ratjen and the Rakoll chemical plant were also served. Between the DB and BHE tracks were the sheds of the H.A.Gründahl fertiliser company.

Right in the west was another siding from the BHE main line connecting to the 'Pikanta' company which processed cucumbers and other fruits here. After the company went bankrupt in 1971, the plant was taken over by the United International Sales Organization (Vivo), which continued to use rail transport for a few years.

The end and side loading dock just west of the station building served among other things for loading and unloading military vehicles and visiting circuses. Also here sometimes cows were despatched and tractors delivered. Later another end loading ramp was built just west of the level crossing on the south side of the station which was mainly used by the Bundeswehr.

For the necessary shunting a small locomotive (Köf 2) was based in Buxtehude, as already mentioned.

Wagons were brought to and collected from Buxtehude by local good trains (*Nahgüterzügen*), Ng 8674 Hamburg-Harburg to Stade and Ng 8679 from Stade to Hamburg-Harburg. These served all intermediate stations in the 1950s, but from the 1960s wagons for Daerstorf and Neukloster were detached in Buxtehude and transferred by the shunter as trip workings 15581 and 15684.

Until about 1960, fast local freights (*Naheilgüterzüge*, Ne) and even through freights (*Durchgangsgüterzüge*, Dg) were also handled in Buxtehude. Among other things, livestock and urgent wagons from Dollern and Neukloster were detached from Ng 8679 (Stade – Harburg) and added to Ne 5377 (Cuxhaven – Stade – Harburg) set. So there was a lot going on at Buxtehude.

Around 1968, the water tower was demolished.

In the early 1970s, goods services were withdrawn from Buxtehude and centralised at Stade, even though only shortly before this the goods shed had been extended by about 11 metres and equipped with a new office annexe. When no longer needed by DB, the goods shed was leased to a company that still received some of their goods by rail.

Above
**Preserved BHE bogie railcar T175 leaving Buxtehude, 14th July 2013.**
**This unit was DB VT66 904, formerly DRG VT 761, built by WUMAG in 1926.**
**In 1980 it was restored to original condition by an enthusiast group but is not currently operational.**

Below
**Loading military vehicles in Buxtehude goods yard, 7th May 1985.**

Above
**Buxtehude from the east in March 2013. Compare with the 1975 view (p.20).**

Even BHE was still active with freight at that time. The BHE had its own diesel locomotives, including 0-6-0 V276, formerly DB V36 003, which operated the route to Harsefeld. On 13th October 1976 there was an accident in Buxtehude: the BHE diesel with a train of eighteen loaded sugar beet wagons had brake problems and went through the buffer stops onto the Stade road. Two cars parked behind the buffer stop and a bicycle were destroyed, and a trailer belonging to the pasta factory was badly damaged. Fortunately no-one was injured.

In 1971/72, a siding off the main track towards Hamburg was put into operation in the new industrial area (Alter Postweg) east of the river Este. The connection still existed in 2013, but had not been used in a long time. It served, among others, materials handling company Claudius Peters with its own siding. Other companies served until the 1990s were a Schweppes bottling plant and Bacardi.

The general decline in goods traffic led to further closures. The weighbridge and the loco shed were removed in the second half of the 1970s, among other things.

With the introduction of a new signalling system in the 1980s, there were significant changes in the track layout, thinned down and adapted to meet new requirements. Loading track 7, north of main track 1, was removed, as had

been track 6 a few years earlier. Buildings such as the former goods shed, loading points, ramps, etc., were dismantled.

In the second half of the 1980s, the larger shed of the Gründahl company, dating from the 1960s, burned down. In 1990 the smaller Gründahl shed was also demolished.

In 1988, the Birkel pasta factory was closed and in 1996 the buildings were demolished.

On 21st June 1987 the new interlocking technology was put into operation at Buxtehude. The type MC L 84 control board was installed in the former goods shed office building and designated Bf (Buxtehude dispatcher). Instead of the old semaphore signals, new colour light signals were used with the routes electrically checked and interlocked. The tracks were given new labels – track 1 became 401, track 2 402, etc.

Initially, and during construction work in 2006/07, the new signal box was occupied by a local dispatcher but normally it is now remotely controlled by the F70 system from Hamburg-Neugraben.

The old Bf signal box was dismantled while the former east box (Bo) still served (as P190) to operate the crossing barriers until 1989. After completion of the road bypass through the Ellerbruchtunnel in 1987 and the pedestrian underpass in place of the level crossing, this was removed in 1989 and the old signal box building demolished.

Above
**An S-Bahn service to Stade at Buxtehude as modernised. Note the raised platforms. June 2013.**

Below
**Almost the same view but on 3rd July 2001.**

In 1993 the BHE merged with the EVB (Railways and Transport Enterprises Elbe – Weser). In the same year, the EVB began to operate a new passenger service from Hamburg-Neugraben via Buxtehude and Bremervörde to Bremerhaven with class 628 railcars.

Also in 1993, the level crossing at Harburger Straße was replaced by an underpass. A few years previously it had been equipped with electric remote controlled barriers and the locally worked barriers removed. However, the former crossing keeper's house was still standing in 2013.

In 2006, the BHE station building was demolished and in its place there are bus stops, taxi ranks, and car parks. To the west, in the area of the former BHE goods yard, there is Park+Ride parking, and a rainwater retention basin was completed in 2012.

As part of the extension of the suburban railway network from Hamburg-Neugraben to Stade in 2006/2007, important modifications were carried out at Buxtehude. To allow flexible working, crossovers (called trapeze points) were installed in the two main tracks 401 (formerly 1) and 402 (formerly 2) at both ends of the station, with the corresponding signals. The former overtaking track 3 was converted to dead-end track 403, facing Neugraben, for returning S-Bahn trains. From the west, track 404 (to and from Harsefeld) runs for about a kilometre parallel to the main line, and then shortly before the platform there is a connection to track 402, or it can end at the platform as a dead end for EVB trains. The former track 3 has been divided into 403 and 404 in the platform area to allow barrier-free access to the central platform. One siding branches off track 404 for holding suburban trains, and another branches off about 500m west of track 404 towards the south-east on the former BHE main line. The boundary between DB and EVB is just to the east of the point to this siding.

Near this siding, almost overgrown, is a former accommodation building dating from 1928. Next to the station building, it is the only remnant of the old railway in Buxtehude.

In October and November 2007 the platforms were renewed and increased in height by more than 30cm to 76cm. As only S-Bahn trains use track 403, the platform in this area is even higher, at 96cm.

On the section from Neugraben to Stade the S-Bahn trains use the 15kV AC catenary; on their own network they run on 1,200v DC from an outside third rail. In Neugraben station there are changeover sections in tracks 1 and 3 (in each direction). Through working from Pinneberg to Stade was introduced with the winter timetable of 2007/08, using class 474.3 electric multiple units.

As well as the S-Bahn, Buxtehude is also served every hour by the Metronom express trains between Hamburg and Cuxhaven.

Above
**A Metronom service consisting of double-deck stock propelled by diesel 246 005-3 passes Westfälische Landes-Eisenbahn B-B diesel-hydraulic 72 (MaK G1204, 1982) on 25th March 2013.**

Below left
**A Metronom service to Hamburg hauled by leased hvle diesel 246 010-3 approaches the station on 6th February 2014. Note the stabled S-Bahn set in the left background.**

Below
**New class 474.3 S-Bahn trains at Buxtehude station in June 2013.**

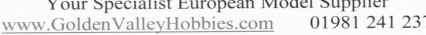

A classic scenic feature on continental layouts

# A ruined castle

**Jean Buchmann** makes use of
a cast plaster kit from Modellbau Luft.
*Photographs by the author.*

Old stonework is often a prominent feature of the range of structure kits produced by Modellbau Luft, many of which are available in both HO and N. I was attracted to the kit for the ruins of Gutenfels castle (ref.N530), dating from the 12-13th century. Its generous dimensions suggest that it was the residence of a nobleman. Even in N (1:160), the model occupies a space of 275mm x 120mm, and stands 142mm high. My layout is HO, but I thought it would work well in the background, creating a kind of forced perspective to make the layout look larger. The only drawback is that in this position it is harder to appreciate the level of detail the designer has achieved.

Below
**The N scale model
placed in the background
of an HO layout.**

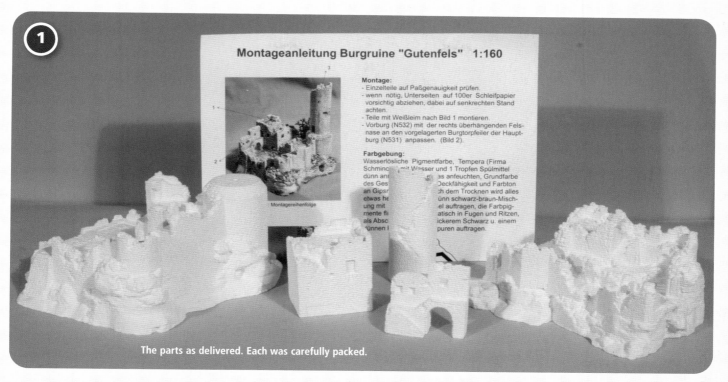

**Montageanleitung Burgruine "Gutenfels" 1:160**

**Montage:**
- Einzelteile auf Paßgenauigkeit prüfen.
- wenn nötig, Unterseiten auf 100er Schleifpapier vorsichtig abziehen, dabei auf senkrechten Stand achten.
- Teile mit Weißleim nach Bild 1 montieren.
- Vorburg (N532) mit der rechts überhängenden Felsnase an den vorgelagerten Burgtorpfeiler der Hauptburg (N531) anpassen. (Bild 2).

**Farbgebung:**
Wasserlösliche Pigmentfarbe, Tempera (Firma Schmincke) mit Wasser und 1 Tropfen Spülmittel dünn anmischen, etwas anfeuchten, Grundfarbe des Gesteins... Deckfähigkeit und Farbton an Gipsr... nach dem Trocknen wird alles etwas he... ünn schwarz-braun-Mischung mit... el auftragen, die Farbpigmente fli... atisch in Fugen und Ritzen, als Absc... ickerem Schwarz u. einem dünnen... puren auftragen.

Montagereihenfolge

The parts as delivered. Each was carefully packed.

A first positioning test confirms that the pieces fit together perfectly and do not require sanding.

The generous dimensions of this ruin suggest that the castle was once the residence of a nobleman.

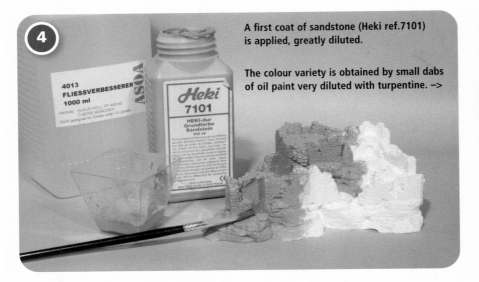

**4** A first coat of sandstone (Heki ref.7101) is applied, greatly diluted.

The colour variety is obtained by small dabs of oil paint very diluted with turpentine. –>

**5**

**6** The ruins in the course of painting.

**7** The application of a black wash (Vallejo ref.73301) darkens the joints.

The various parts are cast in plaster; each is packed separately in protective tissue to avoid damage in transit. Assembly is simply a matter of gluing them together. No major trimming is required – just check the parts fit properly and if necessary adjust with medium grain sandpaper. For practical reasons I prefer to stick the parts together after painting.

The realistic rendering of the stones, the clear definition of the features, and the attention to detail even in such a small scale all underline the expertise of the producer.

The parts are supplied in plain plaster, allowing the modeller to choose the colour – sandstone, limestone, granite, etc. In keeping with my layout theme, I chose sandstone.

All the parts were first covered with a coat of sandstone paint (Heki ref.7101) greatly diluted and extended with a wetting agent (ASOA ref.4003) to break the surface tension, thus allowing the paint to flow into the many crevices.

The next step is to bring out the many shades of colour in the sandstone. I applied oil paint much diluted with turpentine in small strokes to reproduce shades of grey, red, brown, and pink. The colours (Indian yellow, natural umber, burnt umber, cadmium red, and titanium white) are applied separately, then mixed together in place, to create a diverse palette.

**8** Dry brushing with light grey (Tamiya ref.XF-19) highlights the details.

**9** Fixing the parts together was done with neoprene glue.

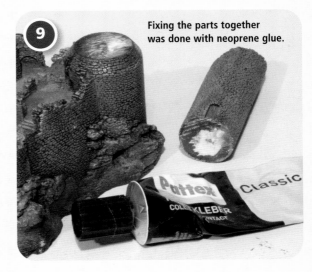

**Right**
**Early days on the new layout. The grand terminal from the former layout has been placed in position and will be converted into a through station. The baseboards are ready and track laying has begun. The backscene is still bare walls.**

al land with new towns such as Almere and Lelystad. Elburg itself is a small Hanseatic trading and fishing town dating back to the 14th century, and a gem of a living museum. 't Harde literally means 'dry hard sandy soil' and the house we found had an extension, now my study, underneath which was a very large – and dry – basement, something most unusual in The Netherlands. Of course, I immediately had rosy visions of a new layout, much bigger and much more accessible for an elderly person. And so it worked out.

The basement is about 7.5 by 5 metres and we decided that a section of 5.5 by 4 metres could be used for the new layout – enormous when compared to my earlier layout (as described in CM in 1988). The rest of the room was meant for storage, as our bungalow has a flat roof and no loft.

**Right**
**The Central Railway Maffei steam tram loco is running around its single carriage before going on to pick up passengers in front of the station. The guard has just changed the rear lantern. A long train of six-wheelers passes through the station.**

**Far right**
**Holland Railway Borsig-built 2-4-0 *Irene* is standing under the overall roof of the main station.**

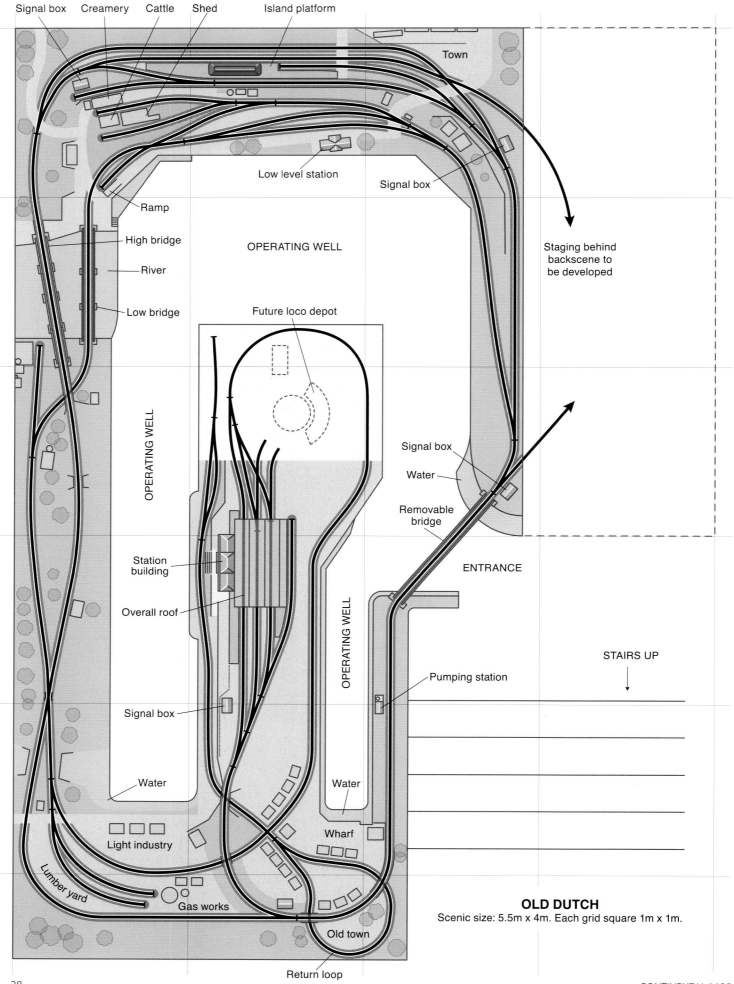

Signal box   Creamery   Cattle   Shed   Island platform

Town

Low level station

Signal box

Staging behind
backscene to
be developed

Ramp

High bridge

River

OPERATING WELL

Low bridge

Future loco depot

Signal box

Water

Removable
bridge

ENTRANCE

OPERATING WELL

OPERATING WELL

Station
building

Overall roof

STAIRS UP

Signal box

Pumping station

Water

Water

Wharf

Light industry

Lumber yard

Gas works

**OLD DUTCH**
Scenic size: 5.5m x 4m. Each grid square 1m x 1m.

Old town

Return loop

My son Dirk and I constructed the necessary dividing walls and baseboards in the usual way, nothing revolutionary there: plywood on softwood framing, partly screwed into the walls with the rest on wooden legs. The single light bulb was replaced with fluorescent lighting, helped by my neighbour Jan Fidder, who turned out to be an accomplished electrician. As can be seen from the plan, every corner of the layout can be reached from a standing position in the aisle. No climbing on steps for me at my age!

The average height of the baseboards is 1.1m from the ground, and as I am fairly tall this is good for working and operating while standing up.

I had salvaged a lot of buildings, trees, and other items from the earlier layout so I decided to stick to HO and continue to use Peco Streamline code 100 rail and points. Some of my early models still have rather crude wheels with prominent flanges, too clumsy for code 75. With suitable ballasting and painting, the overscale height of the rail is not really noticeable. I also chose to repeat the historical time frame of the layout of 1914, just before the beginning of the First World War. The setting of the layout is pure fiction, and no actual town has been modelled, but elements from all over the country have been collected to present a believable Dutch landscape with typical buildings. The Netherlands, although remaining neutral during the 1914-1918 conflict, was one of the first countries to mobilise its armed forces in 1914 and so soldiers and military equipment are visible on the layout. All my locomotives and rolling stock were from before 1914 and could be used again without problems.

I have toyed with the idea of switching over to DCC but in the end decided against it, despite the obvious advantages. Most of my very small scratchbuilt locos simply have no place for the decoder, or if it were possible at all, I would have to cut them open to install a decoder. So old-fashioned DC remained the thing for me.

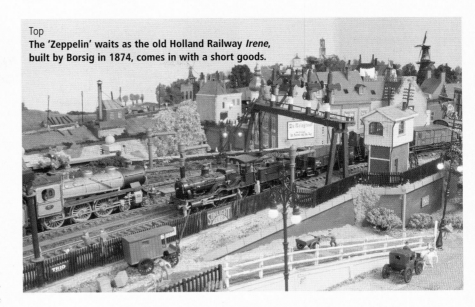

Top
**The 'Zeppelin' waits as the old Holland Railway *Irene*, built by Borsig in 1874, comes in with a short goods.**

Below
**The old town.**

Below
**A quiet corner of the layout, with light industry and a lumber yard on the edge of town. Pollution of the canals and rivers was still unknown and the fishermen are having a good day. The swans are not disturbed by the presence of the boys.**

## Historical overview

As elsewhere, railways in The Netherlands were constructed piecemeal. The first was the Holland Railway of 1839 with its line – to Brunellian broad gauge – between Amsterdam and Haarlem, later extended to Rotterdam, still broad gauge. The Netherlands Rhenish Railway built Amsterdam – Utrecht – Arnhem, also broad gauge, later narrowed to standard when an extension to the Prussian network was completed. The Holland company narrowed its line in 1866.

When construction of more lines came to a halt, partly because of the high cost of the necessary bridges across the great rivers of Rhine, Waal, and Meuse, the government stepped in and constructed a nationwide network. The actual running of the traffic was left to a private company with a long name but known as State Railways for short. It should be remembered that this was a private company too, just as the Holland, the Rhenish, and the Central, the latter also beginning in the 1860s. The big river bridges constructed with public money were the wonders of the world. The

bridge across the Lek River near Culemborg was for years the longest single span in the world and the mile-long Moerdijk bridge was the longest in Europe for decades.

Regional railways with a simpler and cheaper way of running came in the 1870s and 1880s to fill in the main line network, and steam trams ran into even the remotest corners of the country. Some of these tramways were no small affairs: the Limburg Steam Tram Company in the south of Dutch Limburg even ran a 0-6-6-0 Garratt (see CM March/April 1983).

To end the disastrous competition between the several railway companies, the government ordered a closer cooperation during the First World War, when the cost of coal and all materials was rocketing. Since 1917, the several companies operated as Nederlandse Spoorwegen, Netherlands Railways, although the new chartered company of that name only started life on 1st January 1938, when the still existing old corporations were dissolved. Since then the railways have been wholly government owned.

Electrification started in 1908 and has materially changed the picture of railway operations in the country, as all major lines and even a lot of the minor ones are now under the wires.

## Track and electrics

After our move to 't Harde in 2007, it was more than a year before I could start on the new layout and had the rough baseboards and bare walls in place. As you will know, The Netherlands are rather flat and with a lot of rivers, inland seas, and lakes, so water was essential to catch the character of the country. I made the same choice as before with the operating areas simulating the river and other streams, with a removable lattice girder bridge for entering the layout room. When everything is running, you have to duck under to enter, but it is easy to take the bridge out and get access for standing humans, something that might come in handy in the future.

Below

**The Central Railway 'Zeppelin' has just crossed the high bridge over the river with its train of six-wheelers, with the light railway underneath. The big rice hulling factory on the left has its own siding and a private wharf on the river.**

My daughter-in-law Simone offered to paint the backscenes, blue sky above and lighter blue at the level of the horizon, with some clouds here and there, all done in acrylics. And very well done in my opinion. Some hillocks with trees, green in the foreground and greyish in the distance, were added to give some depth to the whole. I think that she has succeeded quite well in giving an idea of distance, although in some areas the board is only between 200 and 300mm wide. Trees, hedges, fences, and some buildings help to hide the transition from horizontal layout to the vertical backscene.

At this time the layout is electrically a single large loop, with the trains traversing the peninsula in the middle, or, if in a hurry, taking the cut-off to avoid the large station. A regional line, 'Lokaalspoor', is finished but still runs on the main transformer. In future it will be possible to operate it independently. The steam tram is electrically separated from the other lines and has its own ancient H&M transformer.

Above left
**A State Railways local train slows for a stop at the halt. The chimney sweeps with the ladder seem to be following the hearse but are just on their way to the next job – not the cemetery on the hillside.**

Above
**A State Railways 0-6-0T with a local train crossing the river on the low bridge. The first two coaches are on the swing bridge section. The fixed spans of the high level bridge are behind and the road bridge is beyond that, partly modelled and partly painted on the backscene.**

Left
**Holland Railway 0-6-0T shunting in the small goods yard of the light railway line. The yard will soon be full of military traffic when mobilisation of The Netherlands army is announced. Some readers may recognise the furniture van on a railway wagon in the yard, the subject of an article in CM many years ago. On the hill beyond is the grand 'Huis te Glimmen'.**

Behind the backdrop on one side three tracks have been laid as staging to take complete trains. The entrances/exits for these lines are hidden behind trees and signal boxes as best as possible and are rather inconspicuous. Not the usual tunnel portal here, as there were no tunnels in the country at the time. The rails and points for these storage tracks are in place but still have to be connected to the control panel, and some way has to be found to give the operator a view of what is happening behind the backscene. A mirror against the ceiling, or maybe even a video camera?

All points, mostly Peco electrofrog, are hand operated for the time being, apart from the few that are out of reach. These have simple Peco point motors well hidden inside buildings. With my hand-held controller, I can run the trains while at the same time setting the points.

The track has been ballasted in the usual way, with the space between the sleepers well covered with ballast. In former times tracks were generally ballasted to a higher level than nowadays. I used ballast in several colours from Woodland Scenics, Busch, and Faller, held with diluted wood glue. A tedious process but well worth the time. After everything had dried out, I painted the rails with Humbrol dark brown mixed with some black. I have tried to make the differences between main line track and sidings visible with several different kinds of ballast. Some sidings only have sand with a bit of gravel, main lines better gravel or even rock ballast. There are also a few places with no ballast at all, while track workers are cleaning up the old gravel and supplying new. New sleepers are also put in place and the old worn out ones discarded.

## Stations and buildings

All the station buildings came from the earlier layout. The centre piece on the peninsula in the middle of the layout is the large 'Waterstaat' building in the style of the 1860s, with its overall roof, originally a terminus but now reworked into a through station. Dirk and I managed to saw it out of the original layout without serious damage and it survived the move to its new surroundings quite well. The construction of this station with the overall roof was described in the March 1992 CM.

The town served by this station is largely in the background but a standard gauge steam tramway connects the station with the city, running through the narrow streets as was common in the old days. Most houses here are either scratchbuilt from cardboard or very much modified plastic kits. The windmills and tall church tower are copies of photographs in books, suitably enlarged or reduced in size, weathered, and glued on the backdrop. Quite convincing, I think, and easy to create a townscape with depth this way.

The other, much smaller town is served by a simple station on the main line, a building on an island platform as formerly popular with the old Rhenish Railway.

On the lower level on the regional line is another 'Waterstaat' station from the 1860s, this time the smallest version of Class 5.

All these buildings have been constructed from cardboard, well braced inside and painted inside and outside to prevent warping. By now some of them are more than thirty years old and still in good shape. The goods yard serves a small iron foundry, a creamery, and a cattle dock. The raised goods

platform will soon be used for loading guns and military equipment for transportation to the frontiers of the country.

The small town itself consists of one main street with houses from several kits, modified to represent Dutch prototypes, and some scratchbuilt structures. Low relief houses against the backdrop are also made from cardboard.

All other buildings on the layout are either kitbashed plastic kits or constructed from cardboard or styrene sheet. Nothing is straight from the box, and even largely unmodified kits have been repainted with Humbrol matt paints to get rid of the sheen of the plastic.

Since the marvellous Artitec kits of Dutch prototypes have become available, I have used some of them here.

The manor house in the corner is a copy of the 'Huis te Glimmen', south of Groningen, constructed by a very dear friend, now deceased, who lived nearby.

The bridges are a mixture of plastic kits, heavily modified and adapted to each site, with card or wood supports for the piers, suitably covered with brick and stone paper or plastic sheet where appropriate. Quaysides are also card covered with plastic stone or brick sheets. All wooden pilings and trestle work on the quays are made from real wood, suitably painted and weathered.

Signalling is still rudimentary, but what is in place is based on the system as developed by the State Railways in the late 19th century. Most masts are from wooden dowel or – bet-

Below left
**The station building on the light railway, a 'Waterstaat' class 5 building, the smallest type built as a result of the Railway Law of 1860.**

Left
**The regional railway station, with a State Railways 0-6-0T and train standing at the single platform.**
**The island platform for the through lines is on a higher level in the background.**

Below
**A Holland Railway regional train entering the low level station. The 0-6-0T is a Liliput Swiss 'Tigerli' suitably reworked. The level crossing barriers have been closed. On the main line, at the higher level, a train must also be expected as the barriers there (behind the water tank) are also down.**

ter – from two diameters of brass tube, with the semaphore arms cut from styrene sheet. Only the larger gantries are made from brass strip and one, at least 40 years old by now, from very fine cardboard strips. They are non-functional but can be operated manually. The signals now standing came from the earlier layouts, but the signal bridge spanning the approach tracks on one side of the main station was made recently from old rail and wooden supports, with the semaphores from styrene.

Level crossings are generally home made, but some barriers from Busch have been used, at least for the time being.

Shipping is still in its infancy. One long barge has been cut in half and both stern and stem are used in different places under the road bridge close to the backscene to give an idea of busy river traffic.

### Locomotives and rolling stock

As very few old Dutch steam locomotives were commercially available at an affordable price, I had to make my own, and so nearly all the steam locomotives are home-made, generally on commercial mechanisms but with new superstructures made from styrene and plastic tubing. Over the years I have described the construction of many of my steam locomotives in CM.

It was possible to adapt some German and Austrian engines, such as the Fleischmann Prussian T3 and the Liliput Swiss 'Tigerli', to Dutch outline by adding or removing some typical parts and painting them in the appropriate liveries.

A few visiting Prussian engines from over the border are by Fleischmann. Despite the threat of war, the international trains to and from Germany and Belgium/France are still running, and foreign locomotives can still be spotted at the border stations. I would like to have an ancient Belgian 2-4-2 'Columbia' with the characteristic square funnel at an affordable price to bring the morning express from Paris in to Roosendaal. My time frame is still too early for the massive influx of Belgian refugees in October 1914 during the siege of Antwerp by the German armies. More than a million refugees then crossed the border in a few weeks, most by train or steam tram by way of Roosendaal, and all resources were needed to house and feed them. And that on top of a total Dutch population of only 6 million! Many Belgian trains were sent inland, locomotives and all, to empty barracks all over the country, and many Belgian locomotives were stabled in The Netherlands until the end of hostilities in 1918.

Most locos on my layout, even the ancient ones, are in good condition and well cleaned. Engine cleaners were cheap and were employed at all sheds so locomotives were kept really clean and shining. And what a rainbow of colours was presented by the ordinary daily trains! The State Railways used a light green with red-brown underframes, culminating in the 4-6-0s later known as the 3700 series of Netherlands Railways. One of these is preserved at the Utrecht Railway Museum. I have not yet been able to afford the beautiful Artitec model of one of them, but I am still hoping to pick one up at a fair sometime. I have to make do with a predecessor from 1899, the 4-4-2 Atlantic meant for the Flushing expresses but a grave disappointment in actual service. My model was scratchbuilt from plasticard with Romford wheels and two Tenshodo 'Spuds' under the weighted tender for power. It really runs well, better than the original, and is an impressive sight on the line.

The Holland Railway painted its engines in a darker shade of green. The very modern 4-4-0s from Schwartzkopff of Berlin generally hauled the more prestigious expresses, such as the international trains for Hamburg, Berlin, Scandinavia, and Russia, in co-operation with the Great Eastern by way of the packet service from Harwich to the Hook of Holland. My model was built on a Hornby underframe with new superstructure and tender. Although finished in a fairly unattractive dark green with black lining, it still makes a pleasant impression on the layout.

Older is *Irene*, a 2-4-0 built by Borsig back in 1874 but still around in 1914. This is the first locomotive that I constructed completely from brass sheet and tubing, all soldered and superglued together. The tender is driven by an American six-wheel diesel bogie and it runs quite well, although it can handle only a few wagons.

More attractive were the locos of the smaller companies. The Central painted everything in an almost exact copy of Stroudley's 'improved engine green' of the London, Brighton, & South Coast, better known as yellow ochre, with elaborate lining in green, white, and red. I have quite a few of them in this style, culminating in the beautiful 'Zeppelin' 4-6-0 from Maffei of Munich, built to haul the heavy Utrecht – Zwolle – Groningen expresses. They have been clocked with trains of twenty carriages, 630 tonnes, and they kept time with these loads. And to think that a century ago these jewels passed my present home town several times every day! My model is based on a Roco Prussian S10, with a new superstructure of plastic sheet and cast metal parts, painted in yellow ochre.

For the international (London – Queenborough or Folkestone) – Flushing – Berlin expresses, the North Brabant Company ordered heavy 4-6-0 engines from Beyer, Peacock

Right

**A *Blikken Tinus*, as the splendid 4-4-0s of the Holland Railway were nick-named, heading an inter-national express on the main line while a State Railways 2-4-0T is hauling a train of insulated margarine and butter vans on the local line. This traffic was common in Holland in 1914, and even in Germany there were similar factories, as shown here by the leading van used by the 'Holland Association' from Cleve (Kleef in Dutch), just across the border in Germany.**

& Company of Manchester and had them painted dark blue with red wheels. The well-known English author and railway enthusiast C.Hamilton Ellis in his book *The Engines that Passed* declared his love for them and their gorgeous livery, as it was almost Great Eastern! After 1914 their work was over when the international expresses ceased running.

Rolling stock is easier to adapt from German prototypes. The State Railways, although English in their locomotives, leaned much on Prussian expertise in the field of passenger and freight stock and most were definitely Prussian looking. And of course, all rolling stock had to follow the regulations of the Verein Mitteleuropäische Eisenbahnverwaltungen for buffers, couplings, brakes, and such to allow them on the rails of all European railway authorities. All the Dutch compa-nies were members of this association. In particular, the bogie carriages introduced by the State company in the late 1890s and early 1900s were near copies of Prussian exam-ples, at least outwardly, so it was easy to use Fleischmann or Roco stock and repaint and reletter them.

The suburban bogie coaches of the Central with their attractive teak bodies, clerestory roofs, and brass gates on the end platforms were adapted from a Spanish kit, and the six-wheeler was made out of a shortened similar kit on an underframe by Roco. With the yellow 4-4-0T at its head, this train makes a good impression on potential travellers. It still needs a brake van of Central pattern.

Some local coaches of the Holland Railway had to be scratchbuilt on commercial underframes as nothing similar was available commercially.

For freight stock, the same German influence is visible, with the very Prussian-looking iron coal trucks much in evi-dence. The Holland Railway had more originality so it required more kitbashing to get acceptable goods stock. White painted vans used by Dutch breweries, creameries, and meat packers have been mass-produced by several firms and are in evidence on the layout.

### What remains to be done

Of course, the first thing to do now is to finish the locomo-tive servicing facilities. I have a Peco turntable to be installed in the opening left for the purpose, and two large engine sheds from the former layout only need some refurbishing

Far left

**The NBDS 'Blue Brabantian' coming down from the river crossing. The two leading carriages are Fleischmann products suitably altered to resemble Dutch prototypes. The clerestory roof of the second carriage has been removed and replaced with a flat roof, with the necessary ventilators. A dining car of the famous Wagons Lits company is the third coach in the train.**

and a repaint before they can be positioned. A coaling stage will have to be made and water tanks added.

More signals to the State Railways pattern will have to be installed. This time I will construct them from brass tubing because the wooden dowels hitherto used have a tendency to break upon involuntary contact with an elbow. This will also mean some kind of mass production of semaphore arms from styrene sheet.

I have a Bachmann 2-4-2T of the Lancashire & Yorkshire Railway waiting to be converted into an ex-Rhenish Railway tank of the same period. The dimensions are almost correct and the main thing to do is a repaint in dark green with black lining, and the addition of some Dutch details. English OO models are generally easy to convert into Dutch engines in HO as the English loading gauge was – and is – smaller than the Dutch one. Moreover, English influence in locomotive matters was always strong, although the Holland Railway in its early years was a good customer of Borsig of Berlin. Several old Borsigs are running on my layout, but after 1890 Sharp,Stewart took over as chief supplier to the Holland. In the early 20th century, Werkspoor of Amsterdam began its production and built many engines for the Dutch, Dutch colonial, and South African railways.

The edges of the layout have to be finished to hide the jungle of wires and control panels.

Here and there the river water has simply been indicated with narrow strips of painted plywood and quaysides, but in many places the original crude construction still has to be hidden.

In the future I may bring the time frame of the layout a few months forward, to October 1914, to be able to add more military activity and – maybe – a Belgian train with refugees complete with locomotive and rolling stock, but this is still wishful thinking. And there are many things waiting to be improved: kitbashed houses and buildings to be replaced by scratchbuilt items, more little people placed here and there, more typical Dutch rolling stock constructed, and more streetlights installed. It promises many more years of work and enjoyment, as my greatest pleasure is building things. Of course, every locomotive has to be able to move, but creat-ing a believable Dutch landscape and townscape of around 1914 has always been my first aim.

# Chemins de fer du Vivarais

**Jan van Munster** of the MSC De Maaslijn introduces his new exhibition layout.

Tournon is a town in southern France on the line between Lyon and Nîmes on the west bank of the Rhône. For some years, this has been freight-only with just diverted passenger trains in exceptional circumstances. Passenger trains usually run on the other bank.

But Tournon station was still interesting as adjacent was the station and sheds of the preserved Chemin de fer du Vivarais, a metre gauge line running to Lamastre, 30km away, and previously part of an extensive network. Shortly after these lines closed in 1968, a group of enthusiasts founded the CFV, one of the first preservation schemes in France. The operation was notable as the first section was mixed gauge, sharing the SNCF main line.

Below
**A Billard A150D** *autorail* **and R210** *remorque* **pull into Colombier-le-Vieux station.**

Right
**A Billard A80D *autorail* crossing an old De Dion-Bouton ND.**

Below
**Passengers eagerly await the next service by the station building.**

In 1995, the CFV possessed, *inter alia*, five large Mallet tank locomotives built between 1902 and 1932 by SLM Winterthur and SACM Graffenstaden. They also had two Billard A80D and two A150D *autorails* with three associated trailers, so-called *remorques*, of type R210, all dating from the late 1930s. The coaches came from several other defunct lines. At Tournon the locos were maintained in a double track engine shed. Next to this were partially covered wagons in various states of repair. An old office building was used for storage. Facilities were completed with a turntable, a water tower, and a coal bunker. The *autorails* were generally stored at Lamastre, along with a large number of freight wagons. Here under a tarpaulin was a De Dion-Bouton ND *autorail* of 1935 which unfortunately was not operational.

Above
**The local market
is an added attraction
for travellers – unless distracted
by the playground or a game of *pétanque*!**

**LE PONT**

Le pont
des Etroits

Voies
de garage

Arlebosc

Camp

**LE ARRÊT**

**LA GARE**  Colombier-le-vieux – St. Barthelemy-le-Plain

**Chemin du fer du Vivarais**  Overall layout size 2900m x 800mm.  Each grid square = 1ft x 1ft.

Although initially successful, by the early years of this century the line was encountering problems and eventually was forced to close. Between 2008 and 2013, with a new commercial operator appointed, the infrastructure and stock was thoroughly overhauled. The mixed gauge through the tunnels under Tournon and on the bridge over the River Doux was no longer available, so at St.Jean de Muzol a completely new station was built with a turntable and sheds.

New rolling stock adapted to mass tourism was acquired, consisting of modified open wagons.

Sadly the old station and workshops in Tournon are in a state of disrepair and are likely to be demolished in future.

But at least the line is still operating as a tourist attraction though the scenic gorge of the Doux to Lamastre, and seems to be proving quite popular with the public.

## CFV layout

The layout consists of three dioramas of different sizes, and shows the situation as it was around 1995. The scenes have been arranged in a special way to form a compact whole. The idea of the layout is to convey the appeal of the preserved railway in a sunny area, lots of detail. It is worked by the typical *autorails* in the original red & cream livery.

The station of Colombier-le-Vieux/St.Barthelemy-le-Plain is approximately one-third of the way along the line, coming from Tournon.

Above
**The A150D and trailer block the road as they pause to pick up and set down a few passengers at Arlebosc halt.**

Below
**The halt at Arlebosc serves a farm which also offers camping facilities.**

This diorama is 120cm long with a depth of 30 to 50cm. The station building consists of a high and a low section in typical French style.

The stationmaster sometimes looks out of the doorway to see if the train has arrived. The passengers are waiting impatiently. Hammering sounds from the workshop.

Behind the station building was a tavern where travellers could grab a bite and a drink on the terrace during the stop.

Next to the station is the weekly market where local produce is offered.

The children are having fun in a playground while some seniors are playing *pétanque*.

Across the end, the diorama depicting Arlebosc halt measures 80 x 50cm. As well as the halt building, it includes a farmhouse with an adjacent campsite. Some farm hands are hard at work, while grandparents occupy the kids. Some campers enjoy themselves at the nearby lake. The halt is conveniently located for campers to catch the train.

On the other side, the Pont des Etroits has been recreated in a diorama 240cm long with a depth of 30 to 5 cm. The narrow gorge of the Doux river is known as Les Etroits, and the railway runs high above the water. The gap is spanned by an old stone bridge. Although the bridge is very narrow, timber has to be moved over it, and policemen watch with interest to see whether a large lorry will succeed. Holidaymakers from the nearby campsite are down by the river, and there are some fishermen who wish to catch fish for the barbecue.

The layout is built is sections. The other end features a return loop (to allow continuous running at exhibitions) plus a couple of sidings. The overall size is 300 x 80cm.

The scenes are lit from above with LED spotlights, mounted behind valances.

The modules were constructed from plywood with foam sheets to keep the weight down. They stand on a separate frame.

Rocks are made of plaster cast in latex moulds.

The buildings were scratchbuilt from styrene sheet, with roof material by Kibri.

Trees were made with a base of florist's wire supplemented with DAS clay, plus various species of deciduous foliage from Woodland Scenics and Heki.

Track and points are Tillig; the points are operated by servos.

Control is digital, using a Twin Center, with operations governed by Koploper software on a PC. The electronics are by RoSoft.

The rolling stock consists at present of three *autorails* – a Billard A80D, a Billard A150D, and a De Dion-Bouton ND. Sometimes a type R210 trailer is attached. These models were all made from kits by the French firm Interfer. Under construction are a second Billard A80D and a Bo-Bo diesel locomotive along with three passenger coaches.

**Left**
The gorge of the river Doux, with the old stone bridge. A large timber lorry is about to attempt the tight turn onto the bridge.

**Right**
The Billard A150D and trailer emerge from the tunnel and run along the narrow shelf high above the river.

**Below left**
Bathers enjoy the sunshine and the cool water.

**Below**
Progress is better on the railway than the road today, it seems!

Photographs by the editor.

# A German original transferred to Alsace

# A rural farmhouse

**Jean Buchmann** shows one way of adapting the laser-cut kit for a half-timbered farmhouse produced by Busch.
*Photographs by the author.*

In earlier times a rural community consisted of three main categories of farmers. The richest possessed one or more arable fields, livestock, seeds, and fodder, and was considered a notable person in the countryside. Then came the household which had only a small plot of land and rarely a horse but maybe a donkey or an ox. Production was enough to support a family, but the man of the house often had to work for the owner of a larger farm. At the bottom of the scale, the daily labourer was the poorest, obliged to find work on a day by day basis.

The half-timbered farm that Busch have reproduced belonged to a medium-sized household. The original was built in 1778 at Schwarzenweiler in Baden Württemberg; it can now be found reconstructed in the museum at Wackershofen (www.wackershofen.de).

Above and below
**The finished model in place on the layout.**

The half-timbered farmhouse is part of a range of products appropriate for a small village.

All the components of the kit are carefully packed.

The parts are grouped logically on sheets of different materials.

Sometimes it is necessary to open the slots using the tip of a blade.

The building brings together under one roof living accommodation above the barn. The house consists of four rooms: a hallway, kitchen, living room, and the parents' bedroom. A steep staircase leads from the kitchen to the first floor (unheated) where the children slept. The facilities also included a very basic water closet.

The style of construction has many architectural similarities with half-timbered houses in the north of Alsace, noted for the diversity of its influences, so I thought it would be suitable for the village under construction on my layout.

A half-timbered house is primarily the work of a carpenter who assembles a wooden structure to form the solid backbone of the house. The outer walls are made of bricks or lightweight materials such as mud or plaster, protected by a plaster coating.

The Busch kit is available in three scales – HO (ref.1504), TT (ref.8789), and N (ref.8239). It illustrates very well the possibilities of laser cutting to make the various parts. These are grouped on various sheets of different materials according to function: wood for the timber framework and door frames, cardboard for the underlying structure, embossed plastic for bricks, and plastic sheet for the tiles with rounded ends. Some detailing parts, such as the chimney and gutters, are moulded plastic.

The instructions are very well illustrated with perspective drawings and guide the modeller through the process step-by-step, which really presents no difficulty.

The wall parts fit together well using a system of tabs and slots, and require no adjustment. The base is keyed, preventing any errors in positioning the various constituents. White glue is used to stick them together.

The timber frame and the doors and windows are already cut out and do not require trimming. The grey colour of the stone walls can be changed – I applied a sandstone colour (Heki ref.7101) and also repainted the plaster infill light grey (Tamiya ref.XF-55).

The plastic material used for the tiles requires the use of an appropriate adhesive (Heki ref.7597). As I did not have any on hand, I tried PVC bathroom sealant which works just as well.

I liked the ripple in the roof finish which suggests that the structure has undergone a slight deformation over time.

**5** The pieces fit together using a system of tabs and slots for precise alignment.

**6** The tabs and slots are also designed to ensure that everything can only be assembled one way.

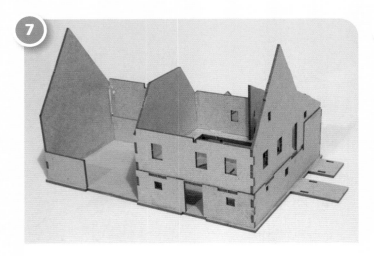

**7** The underlying structure of the building before the outer surfaces are applied.

**8** The pre-cut sections representing sandstone blocks are put in place.

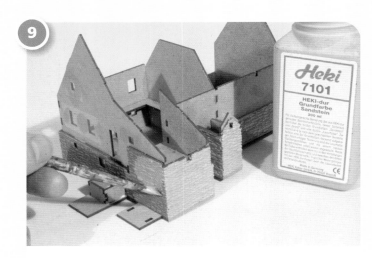

**9** The grey colour is then changed by applying sandstone colour paint (Heki ref.7101).

**10** The plaster infills are painted light grey (Tamiya ref.XF-55) before being removed from the sheet.

The timber frame is then added to the substructure.

Clamps help to hold the timber frame while the glue sets.

The infill sections fit perfectly into their locations. It is best to remove them from the sheet and add them one by one.

Note the ripple suggesting that the structure has subsided.

The flexible plastic material used for the tiles requires the use of a specific glue.

To break up the uniform appearance of the roof, some tiles were repainted with diluted sand, light brown, and rust.

**17**

All the walls were treated with a very dilute wash of burnt Sienna oil paint.

**18**

A brush was used to apply a very dilute wash of acrylic brown (Heki ref.7103).

**19**

Micro Kristal Klear secures the 'glass' in the frames without the risk of adhesive residue.

**20**

The doors of the barn and the stable are distressed by sanding the surface using a flat file.

**21**

The final touch that adds to the overall realism is dry brushing with white acrylic paint.

To improve the too uniform appearance of the roof, some tiles were repainted with slightly diluted shades of sand, light brown, and rust (Revell refs.250, 118, and 83).

All the walls were then treated with a wash of burnt Sienna oil paint very diluted with turpentine. After this had dried completely, another wash of acrylic brown (Heki ref.7103) considerably diluted with isopropyl alcohol was applied by brush.

The ravages of time on the doors of the barn or the stable are easily evoked by sanding the surface using a flat file.

The final touch that adds to the overall realism is dry brushing with white acrylic paint (Noch ref.61190).

Busch also offers other half-timbered farmhouses and many additional elements characteristic of a small rural town, including a barn, a dovecote, a well, and even the manure pile!

**The finished model, from all four corners.**

# A Comprehensive Worldwide Railway System

Offering great value for money, PIKO is definitely the range to look at for beginners to continental railways and existing collectors alike, with a variety of starter sets on offer.

## HO

The PIKO HO Scale (1:87) range is split into three parts; Hobby, Classic, and Expert. The Hobby range is an inexpensive entrance into the world of model railways, with high quality, robust models. The Expert range has detailed, robust DCC Ready locomotives. The Classic range mixes a high level of detail with sophisticated technology.
The HO Scale A-Track has clear, simple geometry and a realistic appearance.

## N

The PIKO N Scale (1:160) range features a modest selection of locomotives and stock, as well as a range of building kits.
The locomotives run smoothly, with accurately printed liveries and DCC compatibility.
This range includes many passenger multiple units from around Europe, allowing interesting commuter and inter-urban layouts to be modelled if they are based around a specific locomotive.

## G

The PIKO G Scale (1:22.5) range covers locomotives, rolling stock, a track system, and a large range of building kits. It can be used both indoors and outdoors, and is great value for money. The locomotives feature directional lighting, and some even have sound and smoke.
Stock from both Europe and the USA are featured in the range and the track is high quality and robust, and easy to lay.

## TT

TT Scale (1:120) is gaining in popularity, and PIKO produce a growing range of locomotives and rolling stock, including the famous ICE High Speed Train.
A good 'compromise' scale, TT offers the detail of HO Scale but the space-saving convenience of N Scale. New modellers should definitely consider this scale, as many generic scenic materials can also be used to create layouts in TT Scale.

Seventy metres of modular layout from Austria

# Arlbergbahn

**Gerard Tombroek** reports on the large modular HO layout
of the Bregenz model railway club. *Photographs by the author.*

The Arlberg line runs between Innsbruck and Bludenz in Tyrol, in the state of Vorarlberg. Construction began in 1880 and the section between Innsbruck and Landeck came into operation in 1883; the rest of the line was opened a year later. The main feature of the route is the Arlberg tunnel, over ten kilometres long. East of the tunnel the railway line climbs 729.2 metres in 105.77km. On the west side the height difference is 752.3 meters but in less than 31km, resulting in gradients of up to 28 per thousand. The Modell-Eisenbahn-Club Bregenz chose to model sections of this spectacular west slope.

The club was founded in 1993 and has its own premises in the former ÖBB halt building at Riedenburg. This old station has been lovingly restored by the club members and is now once again a little jewel on the railway. At present the club has 58 members, including 13 young people. One of the objectives of the club is a reconstruction in HO of the western slope of the Arlberg line. Part of the layout is semi-permanently installed at the clubhouse. This section is about 40m long and includes the stations of Langen and Dalaas. For exhibitions, the layout can be extended with different landscape sections and Hintergasse station.

Below

**Langen am Arlberg station, looking west, towards Bludenz. The freight train double-headed by a 1044 and 1014 will pass through the Arlberg tunnel on the way to Innsbruck.**

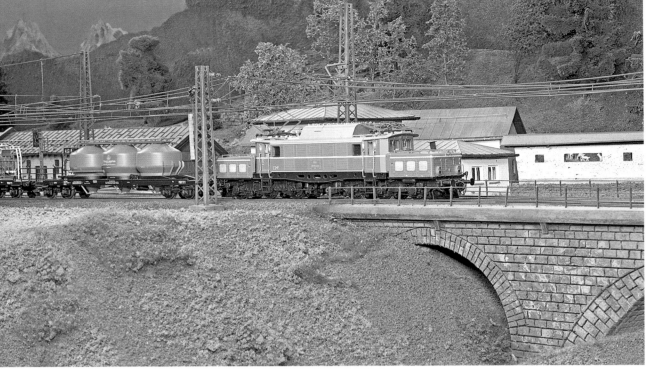

The period for the landscape, buildings, and track plan is the years around 1950 – that is to say, the original single track layout; nowadays the line is for the most part double track.

Key features of the layout, in addition to the stations, are the Schmiedtobel bridge, the Schanatobel bridge, the Rüfe viaduct, and the Röcken and Plattentobel tunnels.

## Baseboards and track

The large modular layout for exhibitions consists of forty-eight segments that together cover a length of seventy metres. There is also a six metre storage yard on four segments, with about twenty metres of track.

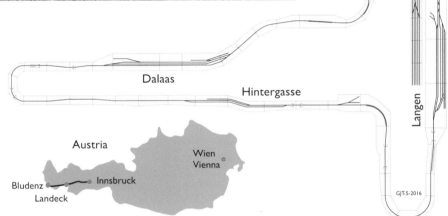

The segments are built from 19mm plywood, and are placed on rectangular beams made from the same material, with support legs which can be adjusted to ensure everything is perfectly level. Each segment is provided with a plug-in connection at each end for the power supply to the tracks.

The track used is Roco-Line; about 130m was laid, with some 29 points, operated by Fulgurex motors mounted under the boards and controlled by Littfinski type M-DEC-4 digital decoders.

The track is on a cork bed 2mm thick which provides some soundproofing. The rail is c.1.1m above the floor.

The ballast used is original ÖBB, broken down to HO size.

The model has a full representation of the overhead catenary, but this is not functional. It was considered too risky with possible damage if a pantograph snagged during an exhibition. But to create a realistic impression the pantographs are raised but fixed approximately 2 to 5mm below the contact wire.

Below

**The path up the mountain above the entrance to the Arlberg Tunnel gives a good view of Langen am Arlberg station. Old 1-C-1 electric 1029 02 sets off with a local train.**

**Left**
**2-8-0s 56 3297 and 56 3472 pass Langen signal box.**
**This train functions as a track cleaner, running continuously**
**in addition to the daily cleaning of the tracks at the start of**
**each long exhibition day, which ensures the trains run reliably.**

## Landscape and structures

The scenery is the frequently used styrene foam and a mesh base onto which a layer of plaster is applied, then plaster casts representing rocks. All retaining walls and rocks are cast using ceramic casting plaster or dental plaster.

The ground cover consists mainly of natural materials such as sieved soil, sand, and gravel. Onto that is scattered vegetation material from Noch or Woodland Scenics.

Spruce, fir, and some of the other deciduous trees were made by the tried and tested method of a wire stem with foliage mat or leaves. In addition, ready-made conifers from the Heki range were used on the slopes.

Most of the buildings were scratchbuilt by club members, since there are no buildings appropriate for the Arlberg line available as commercial models. The basic materials used were mainly styrene sheet and plywood.

In addition to movement on the track, there is also movement on the street behind Langen station building: there is a circuit about 15m long with vehicles based on the Faller Car System. Some of the route is cleverly concealed in tunnels.

## Operation

During exhibitions prototypical trains are run, train formations that are or were typical of the western slope of the Arlberg. However, special workings may also appear – maintenance and measuring trains, specials, and trains of preserved stock. The basic idea is that whatever has been seen on the line at any period can be used on the model. Every modeller will understand that this sometimes leads to inevitable compromises as it is simply not always possible to put together a train that is completely true to reality. This is not limited to small things such as vehicle numbers – sometimes there is just no available model. For many, if not most, spectators, variety is the most important thing.

Above left
**The Brunntobel avalanche shelter and immediately behind it**
**the Simastobel Tunnel; in reality they are at Km 123.432**
**and Km 111.120.**

Below
**You can still see here and there in Austrian stations old loco sheds, sometimes with**
**a turntable. They are no longer used for steam locomotives but accommodate the**
**snow ploughs which are indispensable in the mountains.**

Below
**Among the many impressive civil engineering structures along the Arlbergbahn is the Steingewölbebrücke (Km 119.600). The Rh4010 electric railcar set, here in the later livery, dates from 1965.**

**Left**

1044 100 and another 1044 with a passenger train on the Schmiedtobelbrücke, one of the highlights of the layout, spanning a deep rocky canyon. The model landscape begins just a few centimetres from the floor to show the enormous height of this viaduct – 55.8m high and 120m long.

**Below left**

Loading at the limestone quarry and mine by the Schmiedtobel viaduct.

**Right**

Dalaas station. The Rh1020 heavy electrics (German E94) were for many years the dominant image of the Arlberg line.

**Below**

The most inhospitable part of the west slope is undoubtedly the section between Dalaas and Hintergasse, which runs along nearly vertical rock walls. ÖBB 'Taurus' 1116 264-1 in the striking 'Rot-Kreuz' livery leaves the Engelwand Tunnel heading towards Hintergasse.

**Below right**

Hintergasse station is a short crossing loop on the western slope. The double-headed train moving down the valley will not stop here. To the left of the lead loco (1042 537) can be seen part of a siding – that track is level so that wagons will not spontaneously roll away.

**Above**

ÖBB 1110.27, seen here leaving the Engelwand Tunnel towards Dalaas with a freight train, is one of twenty machines obtained by the Austrian railways in 1956.

**Below**

In 1920 it was decided to electrify the railways in Austria, and the Arlberg was one of the first routes selected. For hauling fast passenger trains the BBÖ ordered twelve Rh1029 1-C-1 locos, with another eight in 1921. The last was taken out of service in 1975.

A special attraction an Austrian class 1180 electric in green livery with a miniature camera built in; the image is displayed on a screen beside the layout. This simulates the real experience of driving along the Arlberg line as seen from the cab.

## Control

Although the track is controlled digitally, the trains run on analogue. Each segment is supplied via a bus. The speed is set with Heißwolf SFR1000 handsets. The stations act as blocks, and between them the supply to the desired route is switched from a schematic panel, made with S.E.S. building blocks by Modelltec. Littfinski Daten Technik and Lenz Digital Plus equipment keeps the trains running via software by Railroad & Co.

## Conclusion

Two 7.5 tonne lorries and a crew of ten from the MEC Bregenz were needed to bring this large modular layout to Eurospoor in Utrecht in October 2015 and operate it throughout the show.

Above
**A class 4010 electric railcar set waiting for an oncoming train in Dalaas.**

Right
**The bridges and viaducts are prominent landmarks on the Arlberg line. The main structure of this type is the Wäldlitobel viaduct in Klösterle, an elliptical arch with a main span of 41m plus an additional section of 8m spanning the Wäldlitobel gorge at a height of 50m. A vintage Montafonerbahn train crosses the bridge – the locomotive is a class 1045 dating from 1927. The MBS had two of these veterans (1045.01 and 03) in use until as late as 2009.**

# A level crossing on a border road

# Camino de la Frontera

**Antonio G. Portas** describes the construction of a feature on his modular layout which is based on a secondary line connecting Spain and Portugal.
*Photographs by the author.*

On the Iberian peninsula, since 1955 the broad gauge (nominal 5'6") has been the same (1,668mm) in Spain and Portugal: before that, there was a slight difference (1,674mm RENFE and 1,655mm CP). The small difference did not prevent through running of rolling stock. There are restrictions on locomotives and railcars because they have different signalling systems. Years ago the only vehicles authorised to run on both systems were TER and TALGO with their own locomotives. Now, CP has railcars which run every day to Vigo (Galicia) and to Badajoz (Extremadura) in Spain, but freight trains change locos at the border stations. At present, private companies use modern diesel locos that are permitted by ADIF and REFER (the Spanish and Portuguese rail infrastructure authorities) to run in both countries.

Proprietary models of Spanish and Portuguese stock have adopted the practical solution of using regular HO (16.5mm) gauge rather than the strictly accurate 19.0-2.

## The setting

Camino de la Frontera is the name given to a level crossing on an imaginary non-electrified secondary line. The crossing is situated to the east of a RENFE station which is near the Portuguese border, so every day there are RENFE and CP trains.

The period is Epoch III or IV, roughly from 1941 until 1975 – the end of steam on RENFE.

## The model

The level crossing scene is at the east of a station on modular boards which measure 4.60m long by 40cm wide. It does not represent a specific RENFE location, but is equipped with elements than really did exist: I was inspired by suggestions and photos in magazines as well as my own memories of trips that I made when RENFE still used steam locos. The semaphore and colour light signals are representative of those that were in a lot of stations. Colour light signals were sited on main lines for train arrivals and departures while the rest of the station had high and low mechanical signals, depending on the category of the track.

The layout is on six modules: four 92cm x 40cm and two smaller sections 46cm x 40cm that are located at each end. Camino de la Frontera is the east module, and the outer con-

Above
**The finished scene.**

Below
**The 'omnibus', a typical secondary line passenger train, made up with a van for the guard, a mail van, and passenger coaches. Here it is hauled by a class 10800 diesel of American origin (General Electric).**

Above
**Renault supplied ABJ railcars to both the MZA and the Norte in Spain. The driver has slowed down to 30km/h because the colour light signal is green and yellow. In the background, you can see the violet mechanical signals – the models are worked with servos.**

nection is compatible with the standards set out in the rules of the Club de Módulos Maquetren (www.maquetren.net).

The boards were built with 10mm thick plywood.

## Track and signals

Track is laid on a cork bed which not only isolates acoustically but also gives shape to the ballast bed.

No manufacturer produces broad gauge track; I have used Tillig Elite code 83 track and turnouts, which looked similar.

Before the formation of RENFE, the old independent companies had different rules: some (such as the MZA) ran on the right while others (e.g. Norte) ran on the left. Signals had to be placed accordingly. When RENFE was formed, it had a very big problem – there were more than 6,100 signals from twenty-six companies at that time in Spain. In Portugal they

ran on the left. On the layout, trains run on the right because the atmosphere is more like the MZA than any of the other companies.

The colour light signals are from the Spanish brand Tawelt which reproduce RENFE forms and colours. They are operated by DCC using CON-RENFE decoders, manufactured by Littfinski Data Technik exclusively for Trenes Aguilo.

They show the following authentic aspects:

| | |
|---|---|
| Red | Stop |
| Green | Route clear |
| Yellow | Slow – next signal is red |
| Yellow/Green | Maximum speed 30km/h over turnout |

Left
**The first steps in building the module. The road climbs up to match the top of the rails. The two curves in the road and the gentle slope help to create the sense that the scene is bigger.**

Left
**Paper templates allowed the Auhagen cardboard road surface to be cut accurately.**

Left
**It was usual in Spain when steam was near its end for main roads to be asphalt and minor roads paved. The wooden baulks of the level crossing have been painted and put in position. On the right, the pedestrian path was built with pieces of sleepers, as in reality.**

Below
**Seen from the other side. There are still many scenic elements to put in place.**

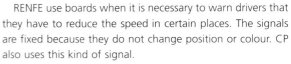

RENFE use boards when it is necessary to warn drivers that they have to reduce the speed in certain places. The signals are fixed because they do not change position or colour. CP also uses this kind of signal.

On the layout this has been represented – there is a Portuguese red fixed signal that warns drivers that before the first turnout there may be a railwayman with a red flag, in which case they will have to stop the train, or a yellow flag, when they can continue and the stationmaster will make them stop with a red flag.

## Buildings and fences

Like the signals, level crossings in Spain were very different because of the heritage of the old companies. Crossing keepers were on duty twenty-four hours a day, so a house was built for them.

I used a kit from MKD for the station building because it is similar to Spanish buildings. Most of the companies which built the railways in Spain were in fact French and the influence can be seen in the architecture of railway buildings. However, all the parts were repainted to adapt them to the appropriate Spanish colours.

The wall in the background is from the German firm Auhagen; it is very similar to walls used by RENFE, by industries, and on private property. The parts were painted the correct railway colours before assembly and finally they were weathered to get the right atmosphere.

RENFE controlled the access to level crossings with gates, fences, and barriers made from old sleepers to prevent pedestrians and animals trying to pass when the barriers were closed. In rural areas, herds of sheep and goats were a problem as they could be startled and invade the track, so the land was fenced. The presence of large herds was common, especially in spring and autumn when they were transferred from dry summer pastures to meadows in the mountains, and back again for the winter. Herds travelled great distances and had to pass over many level crossings.

Roads and paved areas are from Auhagen, again very similar to those used in Spain.

Grass is from Noch and the small trees from Busch and the Spanish firm Aneste.

Figures are Preiser, cars from Brekina, Busch, and Praline.

## Some perspective

The modules are only 40cm wide and it is difficult in so little space to create the effect of space, so some small tricks have been used.

Fences are placed a couple of centimetres from the background, enough to put some small trees between the fence and the background.

Larger buildings are positioned in front of the tracks: this not only gains in perspective because the landscape goes from more to less height, but also as it hides the trains while they run it can make the layout seem larger.

The road does not cross the track at right angles because in reality, on secondary lines, it was done so that drivers had to slow down on the approach to the level crossing. The road seems wider at the edge than at the junction, but it is an optical illusion produced by the fact that the road is not at 90° to the track.

**The red signal is Portuguese, and for that reason it is on the left side of the track instead of the right like the others. It tells Portuguese drivers to slow down and even get ready to stop. Behind is a small diesel shunter, RENFE class 10100, known as a 'Me-Me', with a CP wagon.**

**Assembling the MKD kit for the level crossing building using magnets on a metal tray with straight edges; the walls have to come together at exactly 90°.**

CORTIÇA, empresa de manipulado del corcho y derivados

S. João de Cortiça

| END. TELEE COREMC | APARTADO 14 | TELEFONES 15001/2 |
|---|---|---|
| Corcho | | Cortiça |
| Tapones | Cuñas y suelas para zapatos | Rolhas |
| Aislantes | Cunhas e solas de sapato | Isolantes |
| Planchas | | Placas |
| Juntas | | Juntas |

Delegación/Delegação: Paso a Nivel Camino de la Frontera

## A little story

Layouts can sometimes tell a story and this scene has its own history.

The road which crosses the railway leads to Portugal, but it was necessary to make it bigger. The project included the removal of the level crossing to increase traffic safety, but lack of space here caused the new road bridge to be built a few hundred metres to the east, so the level crossing now sees virtually no traffic – it is only used by people and vehicles to access the loading of goods at the station.

The crossing keeper's house was abandoned, and a Portuguese firm bought it to establish an office in Spain. The company is engaged in the export of cork used to manufacture stoppers for bottles of wine, champagne, and cava – Portuguese cork is good quality and much appreciated. The company repainted the building and opened its office. The company name is Cortiça, cork in Portuguese.

## Rolling stock

The locomotives, coaches, and wagons are from Electrotren, Ibertren, Mabar, Miniaturas Lacalle (brass), Norbrass (brass), and Sudexpress. In recent years there has been a welcome increase in the number of authentic and accurate models made for the Iberian market, mainly in HO but with some growth also in N.

Being close to the border, there is continuous train traffic. Some wagons carry cork, others wine, others olive oil ... the typical high quality products of Spain and Portugal.

**The finished module. On the left is one of the five boards which make up the station. On the right is a module that links with others from friends to form a large operating layout. All the parts of the building kit were brush painted before assembly. After finishing, touch-ups were made as required and the whole lightly weathered. The last step was to apply the name. The sign (*above left*) was made copying advertising which existed in the 1960s and 1970s in Spain and Portugal.**

## A home for Italian steam locomotives

# FS steam depot

**Davide Raseni** introduces an Italian layout set in the 1950s/1960s,
built by Guido Visentin and others
for display at the Trieste Campo Marzio railway museum.
*Photographs by the author and Paolo Visintini.*

Presented here is a classic Ferrovie dello Stato (Italian State Railways) steam depot. This HO diorama is relatively large and follows the same concept as the railcar depot featured in CM August 2014. It is a freelance scene, but with common characteristics from many small and medium-sized steam depots in the north of Italy – the Po valley and the Piemonte, Lombardia, Emilia-Romagna, and Veneto regions.

I am a member of the support group for the Trieste Campo Marzio railway museum and we wanted to show visitors the typical infrastructure used for this kind of motive power which has now completely disappeared from the Italian network.

The dimensions may be unusually large for a diorama – 335cm x 65cm – but the structure is very simple, on a flat plywood board.

**Above**
Typical atmosphere of the late 1960s, when diesels started to replace steam traction in many depots. A brand new D.443 (Os.Kar) has been just delivered. Although in a minority now, over the following years the standard diesel classes (D.443, D.343, and D.345) will have the upper hand.

**Right**
At the end of the 1950s, FS started to test prototypes for future diesel traction. D.342 3001 (Os.Kar) was one of two diesel-hydraulics built by Officine Modena; it was not successful and was not replicated.

**Left**
The back of a steam depot is the same all over the world. Axles and other old bits of steam locos are stored, many in a state of neglect.
Photos: Davide Raseni.

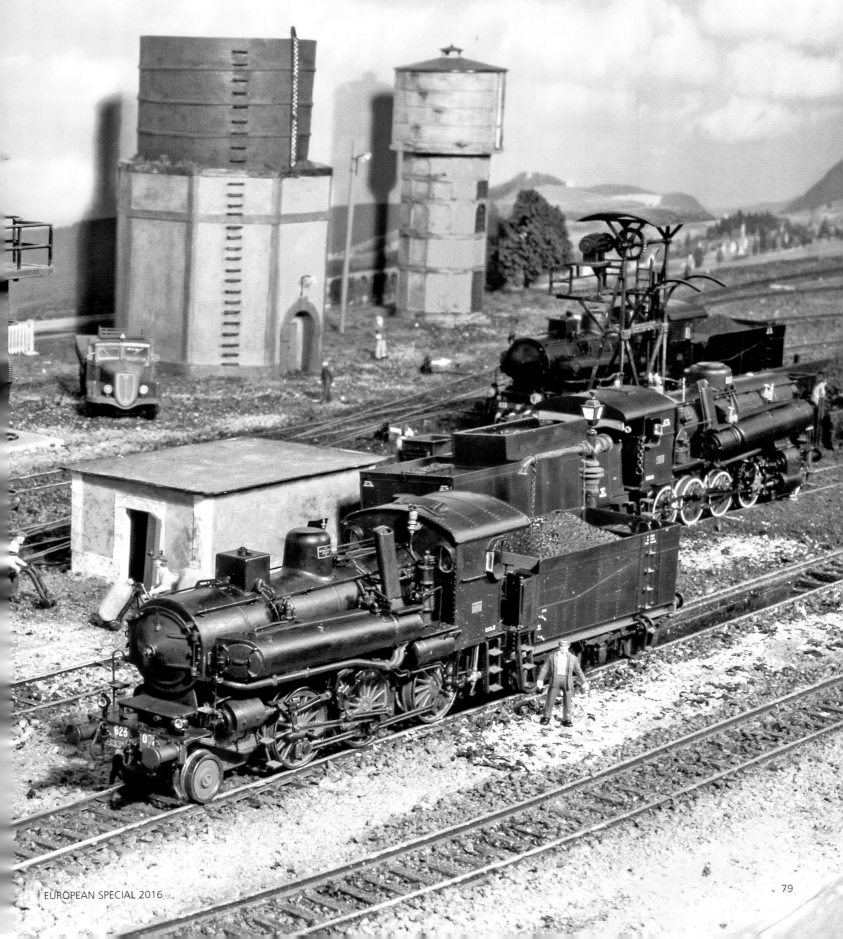

Below
**A busy morning at the depot. As well as the Gr.880 2-6-0T on its way to the station, two Gr.623 2-6-0s and a larger Gr.743 2-8-0 (Hornby Rivarossi) are in for maintenance and refuelling. All these tender locos are equipped with Franco-Crosti boilers, an Italian speciality.**

Photo: Paolo Visintini.

Above

**On the west side of the depot, two Gr.880s are waiting to be serviced. An former DRG Köf, which remained in Italy after the Second World War, classified 213 by the FS (a Brawa model), is used to move the special wagons used to transport ash and other waste.**

Below

**A Gr.880 on the small turntable. In many depots in Italy the turntables were quite small and it was normal practice to turn locos and tenders separately in a complicated manoeuvre.**

Photos: Paolo Visintini.

The elements of the depot, although old, are all still operational and in a good state of repair. We can see the main building, used for offices and flats for railway workers; the model was completely scratchbuilt by Alessandro Finizio, as was one of the two water towers – the one with an octagonal base – along with the modern shed and a few little store huts. The old two-track shed is a modified Pola model. All the other FS elements, such as the sand tower and coal hoist, the elegant water columns, and the point levers were produced in metal by Italian craftsmen and give the diorama the right feeling of the declining days of steam traction in Italy.

A turntable is almost compulsory for a steam depot. This one was built by Loris Cosmini and represents very well a typical FS short turntable.

For this article, we chose to photograph mainly smaller, lighter locomotives that were common on both branch and main lines on the Padana plain with short locals and freights. Fortunately, in the few last years several manufacturers, such as Os.Kar, A.C.M.E., Hornby (Rivarossi), and even Roco have produced interesting new models of Italian steam locomotive classes which have not been offered before, so it was very easy to recreate the atmosphere of one of these depots. Despite it being the last years of steam traction, the locos in small or medium sized depots were usually very well kept because each loco was generally assigned to a permanent driver and fireman. Many of these men took care of 'their' engine with passion until the last days of service.

Due to the size of the diorama and hence the difficulty of moving it, the photographs were taken indoors with the help of artificial lights, and using a commercial Faller background.

Above
**A view of the depot from the water tower. This was completely scratchbuilt.**
Photo: Davide Raseni.

Below
**The main administration building, built from plywood and cardboard in the classic Italian style, with 2-6-0 640.019 (Os.Kar) and 2-6-0T 880.108 (Roco).**
Photo: Paolo Visintini.

Above
**Some small narrow gauge wagons are used to move coal for the locomotives within the depot – by manpower.**
Photo: Davide Raseni.

**Left**
In the past, in many Italian depots, the main building was also home for some of the railway workers, as shown here by the garden with a pond and the woman busy with her washing.
Photo: Paolo Visintini.

**Below**
623.104 (Os.Kar) is taking sand from the little tower behind. These locos were converted from Gr.625s fitted with Franco Crosti boilers. They were used for both passenger and light freight services.
Photo: Davide Raseni.

Right

A Gr.880 and a Gr.623 still with old oil lamps are waiting their next duties. In the 1950s the main form of personal transport for the workers was still the bicycle – the lone FIAT 'Topolino' (*little mouse*) probably belongs to the chief.
Photo: Davide Raseni.

A 'platform' to display trains of different eras

# Gare de Mâlain

**Michel Rouchaud** introduces a French HO exhibition layout
built by members of the Arc-en-Ciel club from Maisons Alfort.

This layout reproduces Mâlain station in the Côte d'Or on the former Paris-Lyon-Méditerranée (PLM) Paris – Dijon line, with some necessary adaptations to both the overall dimensions and the provision of certain elements. This station is interesting because it has a central loop siding, accessible from both directions, to hold freight trains so faster passenger trains can overtake.

The line was electrified in 1949 and one of the challenges taken up by the club was to make properly tensioned catenary, not electrically functional, but which would allow locos to run with pantographs raised and in contact with the wire.

Below
**BB22200 (Roco) at the head of a train of sleeping cars (RMA) just entering Mâlain station. (Epoch 5)**

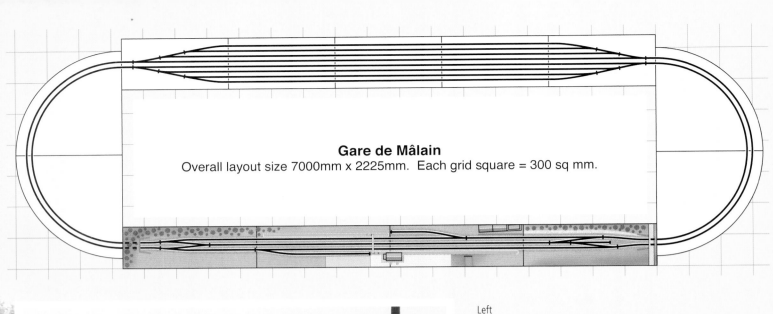

## Gare de Mâlain
Overall layout size 7000mm x 2225mm.  Each grid square = 300 sq mm.

**Left**
The footbridge and the goods loading dock at Mâlain station.

**Right**
A BB22200 (Roco) and a train of modernised Corail coaches comes out of the tunnel at the Paris end of the site. (Epoch 5–6)

**Below**
A BB8100 (Roco) has just passed through Mâlain station leading a freight train towards Paris. (Epoch 5)

The scenic part of the layout consists of four boards, each 1.25 m long, with integral background scenery and lighting. At the rear, accessed through two curves, there are storage sidings so a variety of trains can circulate.

The track is Peco code 75. The overhead is by JV, modified: the catenary itself and the counterweight system was designed and implemented by specialists in the club.

The control is analogue DC.

Above
A BB22200 (Roco) heads
a train of modernised Corail
coaches (Roco) through Mâlain
station towards Dijon. (Epoch 5–6)

Above
The station building,
footbridge to the far platform,
and goods loading dock. The presence of wagons
being loaded sets the period as much as the road vehicles.

Below
An old coach converted for work crew accommodation (Liliput)
and track maintenance trolleys (Gulli Bleu kit).

**Left**
**An old lime kiln converted into a farm building.**

The scenic elements are made in various ways:

– the tunnel entrance and retaining wall were carved in 5mm thick Dépron (a proprietary insulation foam sheet from The Netherlands);

– the two buildings were constructed from foamboard;

– the road bridge is a cast plaster (synthetic stone) kit from PN Süd Modèlisme, a specialist French supplier;

– the footbridge is a composite: stairs from a Jouef product, the concrete base in plasticard, and photo-etched brass railings by ScaleLink;

– the rocks come from Woodland Scenics moulds for the part adjacent to the tunnel entrance and a casting of a real stone for the long flat section near the road bridge.

The backscene was created from digital photos adapted in Photoshop and printed onto matte photo paper.

The trees are sea foam enhanced with foliage of various brands. Ground cover and other vegetation makes use of Heki foliage mats and MiniNatur leaves.

The operation of the layout is organised according to four main periods, from 1949 to the present, mainly of course with electric traction, with trains correct for each era. It takes between 60 and 90 minutes to run through the full cycle, which provides a wide variety of stock, making the presentation attractive to the public.

**Below**
**CC65500 diesel (Electrotren) in the livery of the ETF track maintenance company and ballast hopper wagons (REE) heading in the direction of Dijon. Children play in the stream that passes under the tracks. (Epoch 6)**

**Above**
Turning back the clock – former PLM experimental dual diesel 262BD1 of 1937 on a fast passenger train.

**Right**
Renault ABJ2 *autorail* (Electrotren) approaching Mâlain station.

**Left**
2D2 9133 (Jouef) and its passenger train are about to enter the tunnel as they head towards Paris.

Photographs by the editor.

Above
**BB 44 electric with a freight passes a powerful 240P (from a Loco Diffusion kit).**

Below
**BB9221 is at the head of the *Mistral* named express as it hurries through Mâlain.**

# TRIX

## N and HO Scale Continental Specialists

# MINITRIX N 1:160 Scale

Minitrix produce an extensive range of European locomotives and rolling stock, from the steam age to the modern era.

N Scale gives you the flexibility to build a complex layout in a relatively small area.

# TRIX HO 1:87 Scale

The Trix range covers the majority of Europe in HO Scale, from Germany to France, and further afield to Norway and Croatia. There is also a growing selection of stock from the USA, adding to the truly diverse Trix range.

## HO 1:87 Scale C-Track

The Trix C-Track range is a robust, pre-ballasted track system that simply clips together giving a firm, reliable electrical contact between track sections - simply clip together and get your locomotives running.

# Moving up a scale was a new experience – and a success

# Lippstadt Nord

**Christian Heine** and **Norbert Kicker** had built a lot together in HO, but decided to try O gauge.

*Photographs by Stephan Rieche.*

O gauge was a completely new experience for us. The jump up from HO was a completely new start. As a prerequisite, we intended to scratchbuild everything. In addition, costs should be kept low and not drift into the area of expensive small series production that was once typical of O gauge. The decision to make as much as we could was sometimes a challenge and turned out to be not always easy. This is especially true if you want to build a layout based on a specific location, as we did: we wanted to recreate a station local to us, Lippstadt Nord.

To build a layout which corresponds to a prototype is very demanding. However, since we were only able to reconstruct the station from old track plans and numerous photos, we thought that we might have to overlook a few things. But we became very involved in recreating a piece of original railway history, and additional modules will be created.

Experts will know that Lippstadt Nord was a station on the Westfälischen Landes-Eisenbahn (WLE) and not part of Deutsche Bundebahn. A few notes on the prototype should clarify the situation.

Below
**A mixed goods train from Warstein to Beckum hauled by a BR64 2-6-2T steams through Lippstadt Nord. Note the weathering of the loco and stock.**

**Below**
Lippstadt Nord station. A freight train is arriving from Beckum with many colourful cement silos. The massive posts are not completely out of scale – the real ones were like that because relatively heavy street lights were hung from them.

**Right**
In those days moving a large new television could be hard work. Will the ladies be able to get the big box into the car? It will not fit in the boot!

**A goods train is held at Lippstadt Nord station awaiting the lowering of the barriers of the Lippestraße level crossing.**

The nucleus of today's WLE was the private Warstein-Lippstadter Railway, opened in 1883, which was supported by local authorities and the Prussian province of Westphalia. This connected the city of Warstein, in Sauerland, to the wider state railway network at Hamm-Paderborn. In 1898 the WLE extended its 31km main line between Warstein and Lippstadt by another 29km on from Lippstadt via Wadersloh to Beckum on the state railway Hamm – Hannover line. A station was built north of the city of Lippstadt which had two platforms, a goods shed with adjacent loading area, a weighbridge, a loading gauge, an end loading dock, and even a wagon turntable. The ten points were originally all worked by hand both for running trains and shunting. From the outset, the station had two entrance signals, which were operated by cables from signal levers located on the platform in front of the station building and in the cabin by the level crossing barriers on Lippestraße. In 1911, the WLE built at the Bruchbäumerweg level crossing a signal box to operate the signals and points from one central location. In the following years, the track layout and signalling equipment was

changed several times, requiring changes in the signal box.

For decades, Lippstadt Nord was the most important station on the route to Beckum. Ten people were employed in the office, with more in the signal box, at the crossing, and in goods yard service, not to mention drivers and firemen.

Subsequent history is similar to the fate of countless other private and public secondary lines. In 1975, the last scheduled passenger trains ran through Lippstadt Nord. The last track plan changes took place in 1983, when two points were removed. The end finally came in 1986 – the tracks were dismantled and the interlocking decommissioned; there remained only a through track where today limestone is transported for the cement works in Beckum-Neubeckum. Local railway enthusiasts succeeded in keeping the signal box intact, and as a railway technical monument it passed into the possession of the city. Since then, members of the support society take care of the old mechanical safety technology of the railway. When the signal box celebrated its hundredth anniversary, we decided to model the station as it had been with all its track.

**A passenger train arrives on track 1 and comes to a halt by the station building.**

**Above**
**Goods trains passing in Lippstadt Nord.**

**Right**
**In the 1960s a lot of less-than-wagon-load cargo was still transported by train.**

The construction of the layout occupied us for about two and a half years. As no specific WLE locos were available, we currently run the layout with mostly DB motive power, but this should change soon. We are planning to build a Siemens DE2000 loco and typical WLE type FD60 hopper wagons.

Apart from the 'wrong' stock, operation follows the original timetable, and there is also plenty of shunting in the station area.

## The layout

The layout is built in sections, and operated on a point-to-point basis – fiddle yards are attached to the left and right, representing Warstein and Beckum stations. The scenic part of the layout consists of ten boards with a length of about 12m and a depth of 60cm. The fiddleyards add 2.4m each side.

The boards are made from 12mm plywood, cut to size, and assembled as modules of 120cm x 60cm. After drilling the holes with a template for the bolts at the ends, the parts could be glued and screwed together. Blocks in the corner of the box carry a 40mm thick Styrodur 'baseboard', held in with white glue. The woodwork was painted with solvent-based paint, for protection against moisture.

A cable duct could then be installed in the box to route the electrics neatly. The main bus cable has a diameter of 2.5mm. Secure electrical connections between modules are ensured by industrial plugs and sockets, which are mounted under the boards.

**Above**
**A diesel-hauled passenger train passing a wagon on the turntable. Domestic coal was still an important commodity for the railways in the 1960s.**

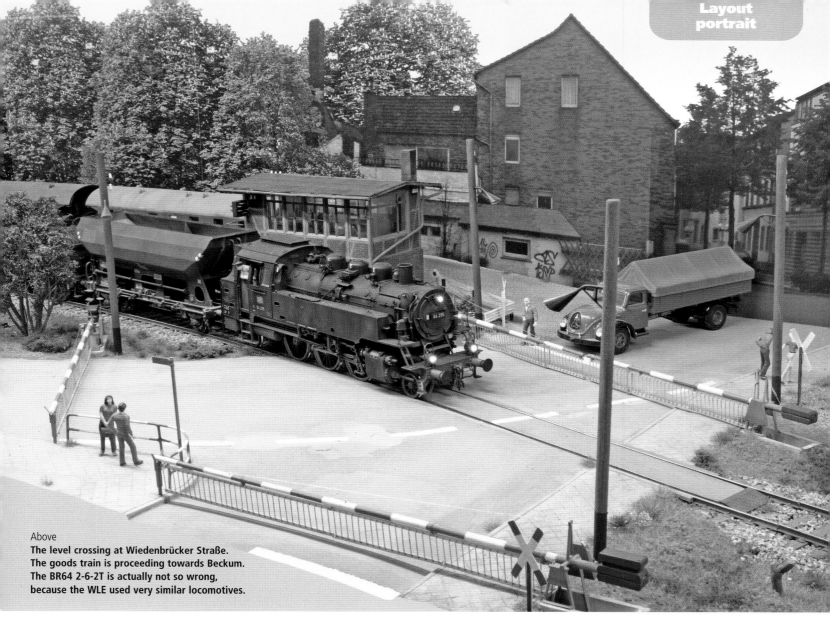

Above
**The level crossing at Wiedenbrücker Straße.
The goods train is proceeding towards Beckum.
The BR64 2-6-2T is actually not so wrong,
because the WLE used very similar locomotives.**

Below
**The turntable allows wagons
to serve premises across the
road. Note the capstans for
haulage ropes which would
be attached to the loco.**

Below right
**Tugging and pulling on the
buffer stop fixings – these
two men have a hard job.**

## Track

After gathering information from various manufacturers, we decided to lay our own track and points.

The sleepers are a hardwood (meranti) which we cut and planed to sleeper size, then distressed with a wire brush to simulate the wood grain on the top and sides.

After laying and gluing the sleepers down with the help of a template, which determined the distance between them, they were painted brown. When this had dried, white high-lights were dry brushed so that the wood grain is clearly visible on all sleepers.

Peco code 124 rail was secured with hardware parts which we had cast in resin with small track spikes which were cut from small staples.

After laying the rail with track gauges, it was painted with Gunze rust colour using an airbrush. When we were happy with the colour, granite ballast was distributed between the sleepers and fixed with acrylic matt varnish.

**A V100 B-B diesel and six-wheeled *Umbauwagen* (rebuilt coaches) passing a Köf shunting wagons onto the track to the granary across the road, reached by the wagon turntable.**

Below
**The Köf is kept busy shunting wagons in the yard.**

## Scenery

In working out the vegetation, we made sure that everything was consistent and reflected the impression of early autumn. The ground cover began with a lot of sieved soil from the garden. This was wetted in sections and Heki grass fibres applied with an electrostatic device onto the damp earth. Foliage materials from Heki and MiniNatur were also used on the ground. Little tufts of grass helped to create a homogeneous overall picture. The early autumn dry leaves originated from real foliage, crushed.

Different trees were scratchbuilt to suit their locations. Here again the starting material was natural. Fine branches from different bushes were used, with additional branches made from twisted binding wire glued into holes drilled into the trunks. Thus we got nice and inexpensive trees. These armatures were then painted and decorated with MiniNatur foliage materials.

Pathways and paving on the platforms were cast with Porcellin and scribed following templates. These surfaces were painted with grey acrylic. When the colour was dry, the joints were highlighted with diluted dark brown acrylic. After further drying time, white highlights were applied by dry brushing, as with the sleepers. Roads were made by a similar process.

## Buildings

Constructing the buildings was a challenge as it could only be done by scratchbuilding. Since the station building had been demolished over twenty-five years earlier, we only had the dimensions estimated from photographs. All other buildings could be measured, after seeking permission from the owners, and drawn up for O scale. However, the limited width of 60cm only allowed for the construction of some buildings in relief, which in turn had to be taken into account during construction.

The buildings were constructed from plain plastic sheet, obtained in different colours from the hardware shop. This sheet can be scribed easily, and cut with a sharp knife. The bricks were scribed onto this sheet using a template. That sounds time consuming, but had the advantage that the prototypical brick pattern could be reproduced authentically, and the required walls emerged gradually. After trimming the individual parts of the building to size they were glued to the shell with contact adhesive.

After the basic building had been painted, windows and doors were installed. These were made of real wood – appropriately as Christian Heine is a carpenter.

The roofs were also cut from the aforementioned sheet, trimmed to size, and glued to the shell. Tiles were applied in strips, cut from corrugated cardboard, with one side flattened, and stuck down overlapping. Finally the ridge tiles were added, cut from cardboard. Once the glue had set, the roof surfaces were painted with different red and orange tones, and here too moderate weathering was applied.

In this way we got not only inexpensive buildings, but also ones which are not found anywhere else.

The signal box is perhaps our finest achievement, with a full interior as per the original, with lever frame, barrier crank, desk, and all the correct fittings.

The level crossings, with the complicated barriers, were a very special project as we naturally wanted to make them function realistically. After extensive research gathering information and photos, we made detailed drawings. The booms were made using various brass sections, complete with the hanging mesh; we also made the bearing blocks and the bells. Programmable servos provide the correct movement.

## Conclusion

The layout took about two and half years to this stage, but like – many modular layouts – it is still expanding. A goods shed is under construction, which will project from the front of the layout and give a purpose to the front track. And, as already mentioned, we have lots to do with specific WLE rolling stock.

Above
**The signal box has a fully detailed interior. A special departure signal (Zp 9) is mounted on the north side of the box.**

Right
**A diesel-powered passenger train on the level crossing at Wiedenbrücker Straße.**

# Gauge 1 on a 'bookshelf'

# Das Bahnbetriebswerk

**Ernst Jorissen** of the MBS Model Building Workshop in Soerendonk demonstrates that large scale modelling is possible in a modest space.
*Report and photographs by Gerard Tombroek.*

Watching impressive 1:32 scale steam locomotives moving back and forth with a lot of hiss and steam on this layout can be a great pleasure, taking you back to Germany in the years between 1965 and 1975. It made its debut at OntraXS! in Utrecht in March 2016, and sometimes you had to wait to get near it – most of the time there were several rows of people looking at it.

Taking part in that show was one of the reasons Ernst built the diorama. Another was the interest shown in his previous Gauge 1 layouts when shown at model railway exhibitions and other events. When he asks people if they also work in this scale, the answer is almost always: "I do not have the room." So he decided to make a diorama which demonstrated that working in the so-called 'royal gauge' is possible in a small space.

The scenic section is 330cm long by 55cm wide, supported by a fiddle yard 180cm by 55cm – under two square metres plus less than one square metre. Such a layout could even be accommodated in an alcove in the living room. And why not? People have large aquaria in the living room, to name but one example.

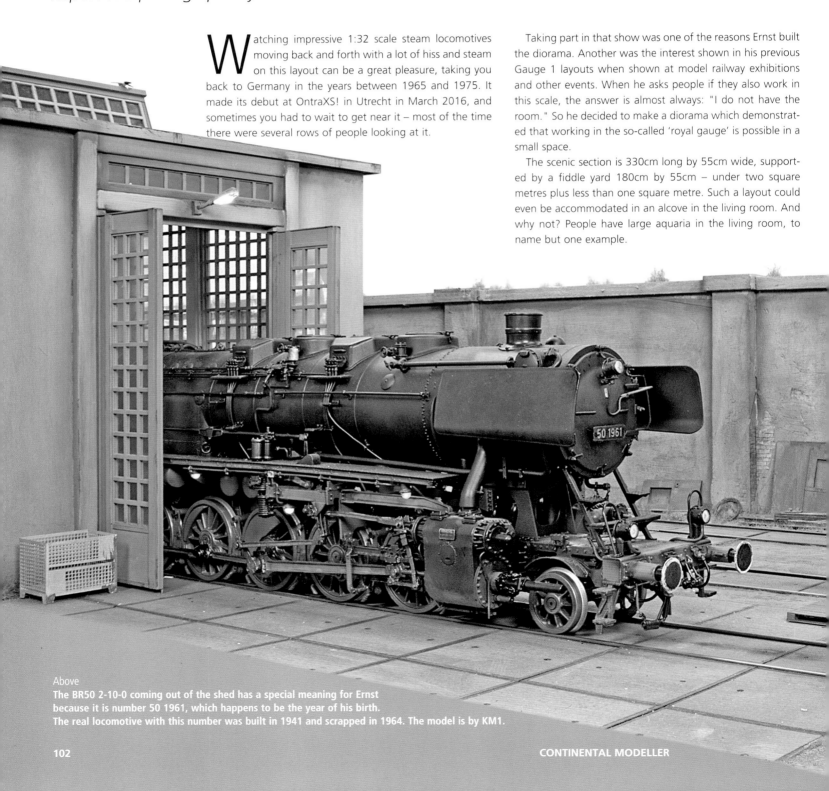

*Above*
**The BR50 2-10-0 coming out of the shed has a special meaning for Ernst because it is number 50 1961, which happens to be the year of his birth.**
**The real locomotive with this number was built in 1941 and scrapped in 1964. The model is by KM1.**

Above
**Two models from Märklin. The steam loco going to be overhauled is a BR91 (former Prussian T9). The diesel is a V36 0-6-0 – these were widely used for shunting.**

Below
**A BR23 2-6-2 comes under the overpass that hides the passage to the fiddle yard.**

## The layout

The scene is set in the early 1970s, when steam traction was still widely used in Germany but would soon give way to electrics and diesels.

A notable feature of the layout is the loco shed with the side cut away. The model is based on a Kibri HO kit which has been in their catalogue since the 1960s. It was recreated in 1:32 with styrene sheet and sections, with the big difference that much more detail can be shown in the larger scale.

The track used is from Märklin and Hübner.

Compared to many layouts, of course there is not much scenery, just some electrostatic grass here and there. The trees were provided by Anita Décor.

Below
**One of the stars of the fleet is the BR23 from KM1 in Epoch 3 condition.**

Below
**The back of the shed, with a BR211 diesel (KM1).**

The wall which forms the background is made of 12mm poplar plywood. The road bridge which neatly camouflages the passage to the fiddle yard is also of this material.

The locomotives and stock running on the layout are mostly by KM1, but also Hübner and Märklin.

The locos have all been weathered by Michiel Stolp of Becasse. He also weathered the buildings.

## The cabinet

To present the diorama, Ernst designed a kind of modular system (which Modellbau Atelier MBS are now offering for sale). It consists of several basic modules with possible variations. The main module can best be described as a C-shaped cabinet. The base, back, and top form one unit. The opening at the front is 55cm high. The construction of the C-shape is based on one-piece formers approximately 9cm wide cut from 12mm birch plywood – this is reasonably light yet strong.

Attached to these formers are the base, back, and top, cut from 12mm poplar plywood. This is considerably lighter than

Below
Under the gantry crane is a BR78 (former Prussian T18) 4-6-4T (by Kiss), still running in Epoch 4.

the birch and also softer, which is an advantage when fixing the track and drilling holes.

The total height of the cabinet is about 75cm. The top carries a fascia strip with lighting behind it.

The total depth is about 65cm, of which 55cm is in front of the back and the C supports.

Below
A BR 211 (former V100) B-B diesel hydraulic brings a tank car to the depot. The loco and wagon are both from KM1. The G20 van by the bridge is by Hübner.

Below left
The electrician is preparing to put in a new cable.

Above
The layout as shown at OntraXS! in Utrecht in March 2016.

The standard length of the cabinet is 90cm, which is quite convenient to carry, transport, and store, but this may be varied, in units of 30cm.

Several of these cabinets could be linked to each other to make a larger layout, or a 'black box' could be put in between them to separate the scenes. It is also easy to attach a simple flat board for storage sidings, for example.

As shown at OntraXS!, *Das Bahnbetriebswerk* consisted of one 120cm cabinet plus two of 90cm and a 30cm 'black box' on the right (making 330cm, as mentioned). Two flat boards of 90cm (180cm in total) allowed space for the storage and preparation of stock.

The fiddle yard is also rather ingenious. The tracks end at a recess in the baseboard where a cassette box with track at the same level can be placed. The heavy, delicate, and expensive locos do not need to be handled but can run directly on and off the cassette, which also acts as a sector plate.

If you want to know more, take a look at www.mbsnederland.nl

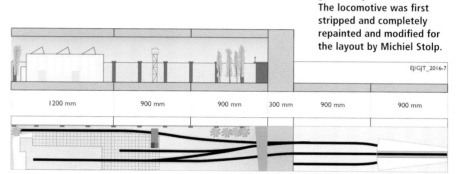

EJ/GJT_2016-7

| 1200 mm | 900 mm | 900 mm | 300 mm | 900 mm | 900 mm |

**Above**

**The 'old' Märklin Prussian T9 gets a major overhaul. The locomotive was first stripped and completely repainted and modified for the layout by Michiel Stolp.**

Below left and below
**Details inside the workshop. The coals in the forge glow by means of a LED.**
**The shed interior lights come from Viessmann and also use LEDs. The bicycle looks like a gem.**

# märklin

Marklin are one of the oldest model railway companies in the world.

They have over a century of expertise, and currently produce models in Z, HO, and Gauge 1 Scales.

## Z 1:220 Scale -

One of the smallest commercially available model railway scales and ideal if you only have a small space, but don't want to compromise on detail.

## HO 3-Rail 1:87 Scale -

Marklin produce a unique 3-Rail system in HO Scale, with locomotives and stock spanning the eras from the dawn of railways to the present day.

## Gauge 1 1:32 Scale -

The Gauge 1 stock produced by Marklin is breathtakingly detailed. Extra realism is provided by MFX-Sound decoders and smoke generators in the steam engines.

## Marklin Central Station 3

The CS3 is an innovative digital controller for both DC and AC layouts. It has a high resolution touchscreen display, and many possibilities for networking. It has two locomotive controllers and a central track diagram allows simple, easy control of locomotives and the layout.

## The railway is incidental – small details are key

# Feldbahn im Bild

**Marcel Ackle** maintains railway modelling is an art,
so has moved to making animated dioramas in 1:22.5
presented as framed pictures in which the railway is but one element.

For some years Marcel Ackle has been attending model railway shows and meetings, and many people will have seen his *Rymenzburger Chnollenbahn*, a 1:22.5 scale industrial railway layout bursting with original ideas and small details, which demonstrates his mastery of decay (see CM November 2010). It is no longer to be seen at shows.

Instead he has for some time been working on a type of presentation wall displaying industrial railways in 'pictures'. Three-dimensional works of art would be a better description, or dioramas with animation. They are animated only in as much as the little train runs through the scene, almost incidentally. Behind the wall on which they are presented, the scenes are connected by a simple circuit of track. Viewers' attention is concentrated on the relatively small 'pictures' which have a remarkable level of detail and realism.

Probably because of this, the attention tends to be held for longer than usual, maybe waiting for the next appearance and slow but steady progress of the little sound-equipped train. It takes time to spot all the details, and imagine the background stories.

This explains one of the principles behind the art of Marcel Ackle's modelling, which in recent years have become ever more apparent. Put simply, the construction of a small object can have a much greater significance. Take, for example, the wooden toy train. At first glance this is just a charming detail, but there is a symbolic message: it could be taken to represent the opportunity to inspire children with an interest in (model) trains an early age. As well being a part of the overall picture, in every sense, small details can have their own meaning. What can we read into the teddy bear, the rocking horse, and many other elements? Whatever motivated the modeller to reproduce them, they can have their individual significance for each viewer. We would not think it strange

to analyse the composition of a painting in this way, so why not apply the same artistic approach to these scenes?

Modellers are generally accustomed, when planning a layout, to go from large to small, from prototype to model. This seems sensible for the most part, but can result in a tendency to fill whatever space is available with as much model railway as possible. But does that have to be the case? This was what Marcel Ackle asked himself. In the middle of an ambitious room-filling project, he came ever nearer to a different answer. With the change in approach from 'as big as possible' to 'as big as necessary', he was attracted by smaller subjects to model. The first result of this 'conversion' was that the large Feldbahn project he was working on was abandoned. More significantly, his method of planning as well as actually making a new project was changed. The starting point would now no longer be a basic sketch of the whole diorama or section of layout but only a very small object, a significant detail, around which the bigger picture would begin to form. This detail should have the important characteristics and fit the overall concept, or at least contribute to it. It would be a work of art which would be constantly developed organically in the course of the process of being assembled from the different elements.

If you ask where these ideas come from and how he chooses a suitable subject, Marcel Ackle can give no conclusive answer. They often arise spontaneously: you see something or maybe a situation reminds you of something from the past, reviving the spark of an existing idea. Sometimes diffuse, undefined ideas go round in your head for weeks and get modified until one day they suddenly become concrete.

Further examples include the broken packing crate, which was once presumably filled with interesting contents, half rusted boxes, the broken plant pot, or the wistful portrait of the woman on the door: whatever prompted Marcel to reproduce them, they will create their own impression on the viewer within the overall context of dilapidation.

There is one other aspect which should be noted. The scenes illustrated here are undoubtedly exceptional, in concept and execution. But everything has been made with basic inexpensive materials and simple tools, and Marcel maintains the separate elements would be very well suited as trial pieces for beginners or exercises for more experienced modellers. Try something: if it works, great; if not, discard it, and try again ...

For more photos, news of exhibition appearances, and some step-by-step accounts of particular features, see
www.feldbahn-modellbau.ch

Photographs by the editor.

# Providing information, support, and encouragement

# Specialist societies

Britain is unique in having special interest groups for almost every area of European railways.

## European Railways Association

www.eurorail.org.uk

A society open to everyone interested in the railways of Europe, whether full size or model. The ERA is exclusively web-based although you may encounter its promotional

stands at railway and model railway events in the UK. The society welcomes all prototype enthusiasts and modellers irrespective of country, scale, gauge, or brand.

The objectives of the Association are:
– to promote the active study and modelling of European railways.
– to do this through the establishment of local groups and the development of an internet website.
– to organise lectures, slide shows, and other gatherings to promote the Association's interests on the widest possible basis.
– to hold an annual exhibition.
– to have fun together and enjoy our hobby.

Members receive internet newsletters, and are entitled to attend local and national ERA meetings, and to vote at general meetings.

## Alte Zeit Gruppe

www.eurorail.org.uk/azg-index.html

Now part of the European Railways Association, the group is open to everyone interested in the railways of the German-speaking areas of Europe. Formed to cater for those interested in the early period, it now ranges from the very beginnings in 1835 through the steam era and right up to the 21st century. While the group concentrates on Germany, it also takes an interest in the railways of Austria and Switzerland.

## German Railway Society

http://grs-uk.org

A national society with local groups who hold meetings in various areas, the aim is to encourage interest in all aspects of German railways, welcoming all interests, prototype enthusiasts and modellers irrespective of scale or brand.

The society was set up to:
– generate interest in German railways.
– provide a source of information in English.
– publish a quarterly magazine.
– encourage modelling of the prototype.

## The SNCF Society

http://sncfsociety.org.uk

The SNCF Society was the first of the UK-based continental societies to be formed, in 1976. It is a non-profit-making society, with no formal constitution – a group of like-minded individuals interested in French railways, railway models, other trans-

port, and (usually!) France in general. The title was originally chosen as the most convenient way of expressing its aims, but is currently under review since its interests are not confined to the French national railway network as it has existed since 1938. Individual members are knowledgeable about the former separate main line companies, secondary and narrow gauge railways, the Wagons-Lits organisation, and much more. The Society caters for enthusiasts of all aspects of French railways and modelling. Membership includes a quarterly *Journal*. The website provides a monthly news update about French railways. The archive and library is available to members. There are long-standing affiliations with a number of French railway associations and model railway clubs. An annual reunion featuring layouts, presentations, traders, and other continental societies is held in January at Lenham in Kent.

## Swiss Railways Society

www.swissrailsoc.org.uk

The Swiss Railways Society was formed in 1980 for the purpose of bringing together those interested in Swiss railways, but over the years has also attracted those with a liking for other forms of transport such as

trams, cable cars, funiculars, and lake shipping. Members include many whose technical knowledge is slight but whose love of Switzerland and its railways brings them comfortably into contact with the historically and technically minded members as well as model makers of all levels of experience.

## Austrian Railway Group

www.austrianrailwaygroup.co.uk

A friendly society based in the UK for anyone interested in any aspect of the railways of Austria. Catering for all tastes and interests, from main line to narrow gauge and tramways, and from the real thing to scale models. The society

shares information, advice, news, and reports on the Austrian rail scene through a high quality quarterly printed journal, the website, and an online eGroup. Some members are interested in the great days of steam, others in the trams and public transport systems of the towns and cities, some in the post-war era or the last days of steam, others in the modern railway with its private operators and international intermodal traffic. Some members collect models or build layouts and exhibit them, others books and stamps and memorabilia; others are keen photographers and make regular trips to the trackside. From the Alps to the plains of the Danube, the many and varied railways of Austria form a fascinating and evolving network. There is something for everyone!

## Benelux Railways Society

www.beneluxrailways.co.uk

The Society exists to foster interest in the individual railways of The Netherlands, Belgium, and Luxembourg, and their rolling stock, and to provide a forum with advice and information for those seeking to model these systems.

## Italian Railways Society

www.italianrailways.co.uk

A small friendly group of around 120 members who have an interest in the railways of Italy. Members receive a quarterly magazine, *Binari*, as well as the chance to borrow from the library and participate in meetings around the country. The society actively encourages research into Italian railways and modelling in all the principal scales.

## Scandinavian Railways Society

www.scanrailsoc.org.uk

The society aims to promote interest in all aspects of the railways of Denmark, Norway, Sweden, and Finland as well as lesser-known railways in Iceland, Greenland, and the Faroe Islands.

The railways of Scandinavia have attracted many admirers, not least for their settings, with operations in delightful landscapes ranging from dramatic mountains, past forests and lakes, over spectacular bridges, and through rolling countryside to the famous historic capital cities. Each of the railways has developed its own unique engineering and design characteristics, in some cases absorbing and adapting British, German, American, and other influences. This results in a wide range of motive power and

rolling stock from the earliest steam days through to modern diesels and electrics. Other operational features, including single track main lines, train ferries, and curious (to British eyes, anyway) signalling systems provide abundant fascination and interest.

## Baltic Railways Magazine

www.railbaltic.eu

*Baltic Railways Magazine* (BRM) is now an online illustrated magazine. Contents include significant news items concerning Lithuania, Latvia, Estonia, and Russia (Kaliningrad region), plus equipment, infrastructure and history. Issues 1 and 2 were in Lithuanian and Russian only with a brief summary of the contents in English and German. From issue 3, there are two versions – English and Lithuanian, and Lithuanian and Russian, with a brief summary of contents in French and German.

## Iberian Railways Society

www.iberianrailwayssociety.org

A small group interested in the railways of Spain and Portugal.

## Friends of the Slovenian Railways Museum

johngulliver1@btinternet.com

John Gulliver publishes *The Cornet* for the Friends of the Slovenian Railways Museum and welcomes contact from all interested in Slovenian railways.

## Euronight Rail Group

http://euronightrailgroup.org

A historical and modelling group for all European sleeper, overnight, and long distance trains.

## Worldwide Group of the N Gauge Society

www.ngaugesociety.com

The N Gauge Society is open to anyone modelling in N, whether British, European, American, or any other prototype, and any era. The society aims to provide encouragement to beginners as well as inspiration to more experienced modellers. A worldwide community of thousands of modellers with access to a growing range of exclusive products and services designed to assist with N gauge modelling.

## The British Overseas Railways Historical Trust

www.borht.org.uk

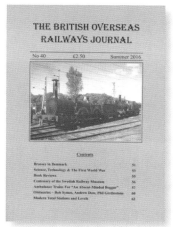

The Trust aims:

– to promote the study of the history of railways in the Commonwealth (excluding the UK).

– to promote the study of the British contribution to railways in other parts of the world.

– to locate and preserve any existing archive material and to make it available to researchers and historians.

– to create a library of relevant publications.

– to establish a museum containing a representative collection of locomotives and rolling stock.

– to work with other groups with similar aims.

## Continental Railway Circle

www.mainlineandmaritime.co.uk

The CRC is a longstanding UK-based group catering for enthusiasts interested in railways outside the British Isles, whether they be main line, industrial, or preserved. The circle's *Continental Railway Journal* has now been absorbed into *Locomotives International*, a commercial publication from Mainline & Maritime with broadly similar subject matter. The CRC still holds monthly meetings in London and Stafford.

## HaRakevet

www.harakevet.com

HaRakevet means 'The Train' or 'The Railway' in Hebrew. Since March 1989, it has been produced as a quarterly newsletter specialising in news and historical material about the railways of the Middle East, and especially Israel. This material is now accessible on the internet.

# SUBSCRIBE
## AND GET THE VERY BEST IN

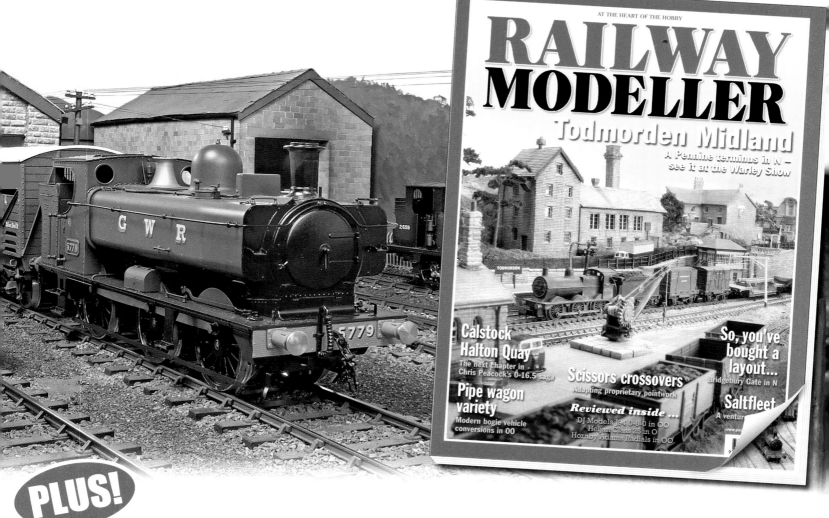

AT THE HEART OF THE HOBBY

**RAILWAY MODELLER**

### Todmorden Midland
A Pennine terminus in N —
see it at the Warley Show

**Calstock Halton Quay**
The next chapter in
Chris Peacock's 0-16.5 saga

**Pipe wagon variety**
Modern bogie vehicle
conversions in OO

**Scissors crossovers**
Adapting proprietary pointwork

**So, you've bought a layout...**
Bridgebury Gate in N

**Saltfleet**
A venture...

*Reviewed inside ...*
DJ Models J94 0-6-0 in OO
Heljan Class 25 in O
Hornby Adams Radials in OO

**PLUS!**

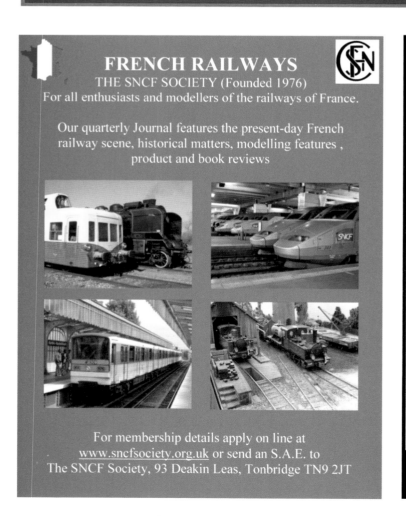
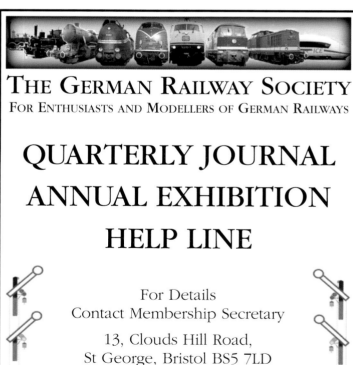

# A pleasant promenade in Switzerland

# Münster

**Olivier Taniou** reports on a Swiss metre gauge Furka Oberalp layout built by Jean-Pierre Muratore.

*Photographs by the author.*

To set eyes on a layout by Jean-Pierre Muratore is a bit like going on a trip to Switzerland. His Rhätische Bahn layout *Rueun* had been shown at numerous exhibitions in France, and for a different project he selected the station of Münster, still metre gauge, but part of the Furka Oberalp (FO) line from Disentis to Brig.

## The technical part

This layout is not completely new, but was significantly upgraded to make it suitable for exhibiting again. It is built on a solid foundation of plywood box units designed by a carpenter. The continuous run layout is presented at a height of 1.30m, on legs which fold up under each box.

Left
**A preserved steam train is operated on this line from time to time, hauled by Furka Oberalp HG3/4 2-6-0T No.10.**

Below
**The charm of the Swiss countryside – a small chapel, Hérins cattle, and colourful trains. The large radius curve by the station is an excellent place to see different trains. FO HGe4/4II No.101 should have no difficulty with this well-loaded regional service.**

At the back is a seven track storage yard. There is no backdrop; Jean-Pierre thinks that a layout should be freely accessible and not locked up in a box!

The track plan of this station is very simple: the main line, a passing loop, and a dead-end siding. The operation is based on the real timetable, in the period between the late 1990s and the early 2000s.

As it was originally built some time ago, the visible part of the layout has Shinohara code 70 track. The points had to be modified to make them reliable.

The storage yard (which is common to both Jean-Pierre's layouts) is equipped with Peco code 75 track and points.

The layout is controlled from the front by a Gaugemaster hand-held unit. The points are operated by Tortoise slow motion switch machines, worked by small switches recessed into the front of the layout. The storage yard is worked from

a control panel with switches on a track diagram to set the routes, with an Acemo unit providing power for the track.

## Scenery: typical elements of the region

The basic shape of the landscape was created using conventional techniques – styrene foam covered with painted plaster bandage. The ground cover foliage is not uniform. The slopes are covered with weeds, using pieces of different colour foliage.

Grazing in the short grass meadows are Hérins cattle, a breed characteristic of this area; these are Preiser models repainted.

Most of the trees were made using seafoam as a base with foliage material applied, but some ready-made commercial products have also been 'planted'. Some ferns made of etched brass have been used, carefully shaped and painted.

There are few houses around the station. The various buildings were made by friends, and include the wooden shed which housed a preserved HG3/4 steam locomotive but was demolished in the early 2000s, and the chapel, which is really further from the line but deserved a prominent place in the foreground of the layout.

## Catenary

The catenary is not functional, and has been completely renewed – this was the longest and trickiest part of the renovation of the layout. The masts and gantries come from a Swedish specialist, Barinmodell. Jean-Pierre soldered up the parts of the catenary from 0.2mm wire. There are removable sections between the modules to allow the layout to be transported.

The various ducts alongside the track for electrical cables with access hatches have been reproduced in plasticard.

Above
**The catenary makes the metre gauge look like a 'big' railway. FO HGe4/4ᴵᴵ No.106 waits for a cross; the train includes a 'Gourmino' restaurant car working through from the Rhätische Bahn.**

Right
**Switzerland is ideal country for hikers.**

Below
**There is some activity on the platform – another train must be approaching.**

**Below**
Veteran FO HGe4/4$^I$ No.37 of 1956 still finds some use on goods trains. Note the weathering of the stock.

**Above**
The overhead section switch gantry is by Barinmodell. Cable ducts are faithfully modelled (*inset below*).

**Above**
Deh4/4$^{II}$ baggage railmotor No.96 *Münster* passing the loco shed. The real shed was demolished in the early 2000s; it housed a steam locomotive preserved by an association.

**Above and below**
**Many Preiser figures bring to life to the layout.
Even the train interiors have been equipped.**

Above
**This high view shows
the length of the layout and
the general arrangement.
A train of panoramic coaches
winds through the landscape.**

## Operation

Services are very varied. The timetable calls for many passenger trains to cross here, and the famous *Glacier Express* runs through Münster without stopping, often with a works train waiting patiently in the loop. You will also see some freight, though this is quite rare. A train of preserved stock also appears from time to time.

Rolling stock is mainly from the Bemo range.

Below
**Furka Oberalp HG3/4 2-6-0T No.10 continues
on its way with its train of vintage coaches.**